Finding Fault

FINDING FAULT

Michael O. Garvey

THE THOMAS MORE PRESS
Chicago, Illinois

CONTENTS

Preface

THE Church and the World are jammed to the rafters these days with people willing to get involved, get their hands dirty, take risks, make sacrifices, hurl themselves at the spears, lead the advance, inspire, illuminate, encourage, organize, and manage great affairs. I find most such folks insufferable, even if they are my brothers and sisters in Christ. Where are the people willing to sit on the sidelines and find fault?

For this beleaguered and carping community, *my* spiritual kinfolk, most of what I write is written. Anyone else is always welcome to read over their shoulders, of course, but it's been my experience that even those few "doers" I happen to get along with make up too prickly and unappreciative an audience. An example: A little while back, during a well-publicized controversy which seemed to pit a liberal American professor and a conservative Vatican bureaucrat against each other, I mentioned the matter to a friend of mine, a Midwestern pastor. His comment: "I bust my ass day in and day out trying to make the Gospel credible to a bunch of Hoosier yardapes, and nothing either one of those guys has said makes my job any easier. You aren't exactly a big help, yourself, Garvey."

Imagine that.

Well, most of what such guys say makes my job (my

7

Michael O. Garvey

hobby, I guess, as nobody ever assigned me to it) a downright joy, even if some of the things they say have tempted me to sin against charity every once in a while. In one column I've come to regret a little, for instance, I carelessly used some unkind language about Cardinal Joseph Ratzinger. I should have reserved that language for a surprisingly foolish assertion he'd made. In other columns. . . . Hey, wait a minute! One grudging apology is enough. No point in getting all maudlin about this.

Finding fault is an activity which is unfairly disparaged. As someone who understood its value once said, "Original Sin is the only Christian doctrine for which their is ample evidence." How much more valuable ointment seems when you think about the manner in which it can be made to surround a fly. How good could an apple be if the worms aren't interested in it? How can we be *felix* if we haven't found the *culpa*? Well, you get my drift, I hope.

Not all of these pieces are my favorites (I have no favorites: as far as I can see, everything I write is just about perfect) but they are the ones to which readers have responded, and not always congenially. They are about, well—faith, family, prayer, marriage, war, children, sex, abortion, television, foolishness, money, madness, hospitality, sin, forgiveness, power, fear, and doubt. Whatever happened to be going on at that moment, in other words. Some of them are tongue in cheek, some are dead serious, and most are

Finding Fault

both. There is even a sermon or two. The variety of their concerns, for which I won't apologize, has necessitated a somewhat disorderly presentation, for which I will. Some pieces seem to belong together and have been placed that way, but that's about it. Most of them have appeared—in slightly different form—in the *National Catholic Reporter*, *America*, *Markings*, and *The Critic*, whose kind editors, Tom Fox, George Hunt, and John Sprague, have my grateful acknowledgement for their generous permissions.

Among my favorite works of art is a cartoon by George Booth in which a man attired as a butler whispers conspiratorially to an anthropomorphically fascinated and apparently apprehensive horse, "He's nuts. She's nuts. All three young ones are nuts. And the old lady upstairs is nuts, too." Together, the horse and butler are incongruously standing next to a piano in an elegant living room, as if waiting for a meeting with one or all of these remarkable people. Like most of the funniest things, the cartoon deserves serious attention.

I don't know about you, but when it comes to the Church and, come to think of it, when it comes to the World, too, I often feel like that butler (or is it that horse?). Like them, we've been imagined and created. We *are*, but we *need not* be. Even if it is accountable, it's pretty outrageous that you and I are here to begin with, the whole situation is pretty ridiculous, and we await with some trepidation a pretty startling Encounter. Most of these pieces could have been written from a desk somewhere in that living room, and I hope all of them will be read as if the reader were sitting somewhere in there, too.

Michael O. Garvey

An Awkward Belief

ALAN BENNETT'S television play "Bed Among the Lentils" aired in these parts recently, a lone program from a series which, sadly, the administrators of Masterpiece Theatre haven't yet seen fit to import entirely. If the others of Bennett's "Talking Heads," as the series of monologues is called, are anything like the character Americans saw so spellbindingly rendered by Maggie Smith, we should all picket our public TV stations and boycott Mobil products until Alistair Cooke agrees to introduce the rest of these Brits.

In the play, Smith's (or Bennett's) Susan gradually discloses herself as the alcoholic wife of an ambitious Anglican vicar in a claustrophobic English parish. The community over which her insufferable husband presides suffocates complacently as she vainly fortifies herself against its conventional and very respectable despair with drink and adultery. There's much more to it than this, of course. Susan is a rich and mysterious work of art, and I won't attempt to describe her pain. See the program. Somebody must have videotaped it.

The eviscerated and sentimentalized belief pervading Susan's story, though, the barren religiosity out of which her anguish flares, are pretty haunting things. If you like to read Flannery O'Connor's stories as much

11

Michael O. Garvey

as I do, I bet that you get a little uneasy when worship gets a little too respectable and tidy. You suspect that something numinous and implacable is going to come roaring into the whole licensed daydream. As one of her characters does, you dread a future moment when some terrifying thing is going to rear up out of the ground before you, demanding that you name it and be judged by the name you give it. You sit in some badly decorated church not quite listening to some endless homily watching thin winter sunlight pierce glass the color of blood and suddenly become anxious that the light might become a sound and the sound will become a voice and the voice will be God's voice and nobody will be able to bear hearing it. You think: How dare I call on God, go to Mass, say night prayers with my kids, What am I, nuts? And—who knows?— you might be.

Even as a believer, you must admit that belief is weird: Salman Rushdie's novel is deemed blasphemous by millions of Moslems who haven't read it but who know that it has violated something, the memory of the Prophet, which is sacred. Before he died, Ayatollah Khomeni said that Rushdie should be killed, and an Iranian cleric has put a million dollars on the poor satirist's head. Rushdie is hiding now. They (the people who decide what we infidels are going to think about week by week) are now saying that the call for Rushdie's murder was a political maneuver on Khomeni's part, a means of emphasizing that despite their recent defeats on the battlefield, the Imam and his Ira-

Finding Fault

nian associates remain the true custodians and protectors of great Islamic causes. Whether or not this is so, whether or not they are being used, those outraged crowds baying for the blasphemer's blood are truly outraged. A sensibility is operating here to which a secularist simply has no access. Whatever else they are, these apparent madmen are people whose prayers are neither halfhearted nor phony. A couple of generations ago, Charles de Foucauld's conversion was partially brought about by his observation of the integrity of their faith.

You pray for Salman Rushdie and you remember the first time you heard that nearly a thousand people in a Guyanese jungle had committed suicide and murder, giving ugly witness to something almost unimaginable. You remember the dullwitted couple in the trailerpark up the road from your house who were prosecuted for having presided over the death of a child, their son, fearful that their seeking medical intervention might mock Providence. Newspapers, car radios and television screens regularly present you, along with more secular depravities, these stories of belief gone hideously awry.

The stories are entertainment, really, for those subscribing to a competing worldview. Those who stand in the presence of a big blue screen and think they understand the Big Picture, who study the *Times* daily for the signs of the times, who give generously to the United Way, who loathe the high fats and revere the high fibers, who vote correctly, listen attentively to

13

Michael O. Garvey

National Public Radio, share their feelings and re-
nounce value judgments, dualities, Jerry Falwell and
all his works . . . those most congenial and distracted
people who confess a creed without a name . . . who
can blame them for finding a sort of consolation in the
stories? They see and hear and read all the time about
death threats, suicides and fatal child abuse, but these
particular atrocities have been undertaken in the name
of God. At bedtime, they click on the remote so that
Ted Koppel can interpret for them some hooples
dunking witches in Salem, a geek schoolboard member denouncing *Catcher in the Rye,* or a blubbering
gristlebrained preacher who's been caught in adultery.
These preposterous behaviors and attitudes, they
know, can be expected of people who have staked
their lives on an insight, people for whom matters of
belief are matters of life and death. It's easy to see why
most reasonable people would prefer the domesticated, flower-arranging sort of religion that drove the
vicar's wife to drink, or the delirium of ecclesial
politics or the breezily secular magisterium of the *New
York Times.* These are creeds you can lean on. Not
very hard, true, but they are steady, and you can lean
on them. And they are creeds which are certainly not
too hot to handle. Lukewarm, in fact. You can explain
them to people who aren't interested in them, partially
because they are so uninteresting, true, but they are
easy to understand and you can explain them.

But when you believe that two millenia ago, God
was pounded and expelled by the contracting walls of

Finding Fault

his mother's womb, slipped terrified and helpless down her vaginal canal, and disgorged into all of this racket and color and joy and pain and death and necessity to have his umbilical chord severed and his fright and hunger satisfied by her milk; when you believe, as you've told your own children you do, that the same God and man is offered to us to be eaten, body and blood and soul and divinity so that we will live with and in him, as he does, forever; when you believe these things and think about them, even when you think about them during the most painstakingly inoffensive, doctrinally correct and utterly conventional, utterly respectable liturgies, you have to shudder a little.

In Rushdie's novel one of the passages the clerics have condemned as blasphemous includes the observation that "there is no bitterness like that of a man who finds out he has been believing in a ghost." You sometimes wonder if that bitterness might not be preferable to the anxiety which accompanies a certainty of things unseen.

You who sneer at the *National Enquirer* headlines as you wait in the supermarket checkout line, you believe and tell your kids to believe something far more farfetched than that message, Elvis Reincarnated in Perth Amboy Transvestite's Hamster, how can you talk sensibly about insane events and conditions you know to be true? How can you announce that we and all those we love and our whole immeasurable and intriguing world are slipping away, dying despite our obdurate longings, and that even those longings are inadequate, and that we will soon be rescued, restored, and made one with the origin of all longing, with Love, the Father of Jesus?

How much happier you might be if you could only be more objective, if you could really believe in the God of Comparative Religion, if you could really appreciate the Big Picture which the howling crazies in the streets of Teheran don't seem to understand either. How can you bear to have so much more in common with those screaming, beturbaned, clerical flippos whose eyes have too much white in them and with those bonehead preachers who quote so idiotically from Scripture in their nasal cracker accents and with those strange, troubled men who staff the curial bureaucracies than with that tastefully groomed son of the Enlightment, that confident North Atlantic-looking guy in the blue blazer, that most articulate expert Ted Koppel has invited on *Nightline* this evening to explain what all the commotion is about?

The State of the Church is Indiana

IT'S one of the nearly tropical and nevertheless exhilarating Midwestern dog days, a Saturday deep in the delirious half of August, when all a decent supermarket widower can do is cordon off his three summer-crazed kids in the backyard, among the K-Mart Coleco wading pool, the sandbox and the lawn sprinkler, watching them grow like the beefsteak tomatoes. A conversation between his four and five-year-old boys has grown amiably shrill and direction-less—Batman, werewolves, Great Danes, clowns and soldiers all dancing around in some psychotic narra-tive—and his two-year-old girl is preoccupied nearby with her freshly stripped Popsicle stick, squealing her delight while demolishing a colony of black ants.

As all this holy confusion and inclusion buzzes around him, he sucks a cold beer, sits on a milk crate and idly rips pinchfuls of clover and crabgrass from a brick pathway that was in the beginning, is now, and ever shall be overgrown with the damn stuff. He's been working at this project, off and on and only on days like this one, for three summers now. He is whol-ly happy, and his hands are as dirty as his children's. It's one of the gifts of marriage: costly fidelity yields up invaluable fruit. Babysitting becomes magic; necessity becomes blessing; duty becomes joy.

He suspects his kids, too, sense this grace. When he

17

Michael O. Garvey

is not so obtrusively correcting their every last gesture
and word, not so assiduously raising them; when he is
just weeding that old brick path that they know he will
never finish; when he is seated on this milk crate with a
cold can of beer handy, they, too, might get a glimpse
of how much love inheres in the unremarkable. And
they, too, might know how much he really loves being
here in the same summer spell with them, an equal, if
elder, dirtball playmate, goofing around in this stifling
and green backyard.

His little boys have come dripping from the wading
pool to make small talk and watch him work at the
tufts of weed. His little girl is now cooing some pagan
hymn a thousand years older than the language in
which he and the boys have begun to converse with
nonchalant honesty. They find themselves talking
about God, naturally enough, who is bigger than the
whole world; yes, who is bigger than Hulk Hogan;
yes, who is stronger than Hulk Hogan; yes, who could
kick Hulk Hogan's butt, in fact; Who loves everybody,
yes, even President Bush (no matter what Mom says
when the news on the car radio upsets her); who lets
there be wars; yes, who does not love wars; no, but
who lets there be wars, because he made us all free,
and free means we can do anything, even things that
God doesn't want us to do, because if he hadn't made
us like that, we wouldn't be able to love him the way
all of us love each other.

His four-year-old boy wonders why God made us
like that, and he has to admit that he doesn't know,

Finding Fault

but that he's grateful God did. Otherwise, how could they, Dad, Mom, Michael, Joseph and Monica, ever have come to be and come together, and how could they all be together on this particular summer day in this particular bright green backyard, waiting for Mom to come home while Monica sings so sweetly? As if to answer, the four-year-old smiles, rolls his eyes, hugs his father's neck and kisses his ear—with a loud raspberry. Giggling at his graphic threats, the boys thunder away across the grass like colts, their skin shiny with poolwater and sunlight. His little girl still stoops over her anthill, still sings a beautiful song to the creatures she has displaced. Her eyebrows are arched tenderly as she sings to the ants, innocent of the chaos she has inflicted on their community.

It occurs to him that he's just been catechizing. That he's been (his mind rejects the spoiled word, almost as if gagging) *ministering* to these children, teaching them theology, helping their faith chase understanding. He remembers other things he and his wife have told them, axioms their own parents had taught: That when two people get married, they promise to help each other get to heaven, just as Jesus promises to help all of us; that Jesus is often hiding behind the eyes of those we are inclined to treat unfairly and unkindly, eager to see in our demeanor some purposeless and overriding attempt to imitate him; that we may indeed be as mean-spirited and weak as we suspect we are, but that not even that matters, because we are worth everything to him; that he, too, was born into turmoil,

19

Michael O. Garvey

struggled through bad days and heartbreak and terror
and pain to death and new life to show us a way, and
that he is that way himself, always there in tabernacles
and Eucharists and whenever we called out to him
alone or together; that we are Catholics, members of
one family over space and time, the Catholic Church,
and that our eldest brother lives in Rome.

He wonders, while working at the bricks and weeds,
his favorite futile project, why so little is heard these
days of that Church's real life; how odd that life must
appear to those whose only access is the news. Mani-
festoes proliferate in the news. Some are for Paul and
others for Apollos. University employees and Vatican
bureaucrats scrap about the legitimacy of theological
dissent from institutional pronouncement. Encyclicals
reaffirm the *filioque* clause, support the Immaculate
Conception, and ban the contraceptive contraption.
Unread drafts of pastoral letters on economics,
women, baseball, bacteriological warfare, vegetarian-
ism and vasectomies are circulating. The Bishop of
Rome, Lima, or Kokomo reveals himself as too auth-
oritarian, insufficiently pastoral, or downright flakey.

Oh, he knows that he is another of these *quidnuncs*,
all right. He knows that he loves all of this idle gossip
as much as the next *quidnunc*; that he, too, has the
craving for extraordinary incident. But he wonders
how any of this hearsay really concerns or affects the
Church, his larger family. What if they all woke up
tomorrow to discover that a sort of *glasnost* had been
implemented overnight: Priests could now marry and

Finding Fault

women could now be ordained; Dorothy Day had been canonized; Professor Curran and Cardinal Ratzinger were drinking buddies; Dom Helder Camara was Pope; George Bush had repented and was now on retreat in a Trappist monastery; the Third Secret of Fatima had been read from every pulpit, and the renewed liturgy was unanimously approved as perfect. What would happen then?

Would this backyard, now humming, then roar with God's presence? Could he then put aside his anxiety, no longer afraid of the day when, perhaps first through the television news and then from the wind or the sky, he might learn of a horror against which he and his loved ones were as powerless as his daughter's diaspora of black ants? Could he and his wife then rest assured that their pretty children and their parents, brothers, sisters and friends were all forever safe? Would God then figure more directly in their anguishes and delights? Would the abyss between themselves and what they knew happened in the Eucharist then be narrowed? Would they then tend less to pass judgment on the bullies and the cowards and the wimps and the yahoos with whom they had to wrangle out a Catholic fellowship?

He thinks how the Church, that molten entity eternally overlapping the pronouns "it," "she," "us," and "them" with the imperative of a cosmic and personal emergency, enfolds these weird disciples who will always be shrieking at one another. He remembers a story his uncle once told him: About Jesus at the Last

Michael O. Garvey

Supper, looking around the table at his best friends, noticing Judas, the collaborator, and Peter, who would deny that he'd ever clapped eyes on him, and the others who would scatter like startled crack freaks when push came to shove. Jesus, turning to the head-waiter and saying, "Separate checks, please." He thinks about the folklore and the wisecracks he might flinch to hear coming from the lips of those outside the family, like the comments that papal diplomacy began 2,000 years ago in a courtyard with the first Pope denying three times that he knew Jesus; or that compulsory celibacy is a sign of God's tenderness toward the wives and children upon whom married priests would otherwise be inflicted; or that you should never do business with a daily communicant.

He, like his own children, was dragooned into the operation, screaming bloody murder in a drafty 1950s vestibule at the cold and excorcising water, spitting and gagging at the bitter taste of salt. By the time his little girl was baptized the liturgical style had changed slightly. He watches her across the backyard, waving her Popsicle stick like a magic wand while she sings, and remembers her exuberant gasp and trusting smile as her plump body splashed naked in the much warmer sacramental waters of a roomy basin, tightly surrounded by pleased and attentive young cousins and friends.

It's all the same really, he thinks. She had not been consulted beforehand and neither had he. God does the choosing and you find out about the rest gradually

Finding Fault

from your folks: How you have landed in a turbulent and global household with the galaxy's most eccentric rules; that the lights are never to be put out and the stranger never to be turned away; that the meals are to be served whenever there is hunger; that the groceries must be generously depleted and generously replenished with everything everyone has; that those who fret and grouse and cheat and lie and steal and kill must be relentlessly sought out and brought back to life; that those who break the rules and those who abandon the house must be pursued to the remotest frontiers of their souls and forgiven; that those who pass judgment on the violators of house rules, like those who take their author for granted, are doomed. And that those who inhabit the household must always remember that what is outside is ending.

The whole backyard, the whole hemisphere, the whole shebang is gradually ending all around him, and so much of what he thinks he is is ending, too, but all to make room. To make room for a fiercer thing, a finer joy; to make room for the author of the ancient song his daughter is singing.

The state of the Church is Indiana, he thinks. The state of the Church is throbbing. In the state of the Church, you can hear the corn grow. The Church is at work all over the ending world, at work on this damned brick path that will never be free of fresh clover. The Church is sipping a cold beer, singing something about ants and sprinklers and Popsicle sticks, screaming happy gibberish among the beefsteak tomatoes, smiling and rolling its eyes and blowing raspberries in a potbellied man's unsuspecting ear. The heart of the Church is longing and full and broken and overflowing today, wishing that a good wife would hurry home from her supermarket errands to have a beer while she inspects an unfinished and ridiculous project. The Church wishes to behold this particular backyard looking clean and fine in the afternoon light; to watch the slick wet flesh of sons darting and flashing through a humid and Edenic jungle of domestic greenery; to give a kind of thanks and to listen in awe while a whole wide universe swells up with a daughter's song.

A Growl from the Vestibule

IT'S an unpleasant metaphor, perhaps, but I think I'm becoming a parochial *contra*. Don't get me wrong, I was all for the revolution which removed the churching of women and the laundering of the lace of the Infant of Prague and I know that one shouldn't give aid and comfort to the people who want to bring back *Treasure Chest* and Father McGuire's Baltimore Catechism #12, but why is it so widely assumed that excitable Vatican paperpushers and the cowboys of American Ultramontana have the corner on the bean-bag market?

Our six-year-old boy is reaching what the Dominican sisters who taught his daddy catechism used to call the age of reason . . . the stage, if I remember correctly, in the development of a boy's wits and will at which the miserable little snot becomes capable of committing a mortal sin and damning his decayed and repulsive soul to the eternal and barely imaginable (but they were always willing to try) horrors of hell. Or, if I remember correctly, the stage in the development of a boy's wits and will at which he becomes capable of a life as depressingly holy as Dominic Savio's or Aloysius Gonzaga's. The alternatives, as I remember them, were pretty bleak: either you become the kind of seven-year-old kid who not only wouldn't mind but would really enjoy living in the exclusive company of

Michael O. Garvey

Dominican sisters for the rest of his life or, not to put too fine a point on it, you fry. And this before all the business about sex had to be considered.

There are no pre-Vatican II Dominican sisters in our six-year-old's life, and that's a mixed blessing. On the one hand, he isn't tormented by an urgent choice between being a complete dork and being a french fry perpetually bubbling in the deep fat of some infernal Steak 'n Shake; on the other hand, he will be prepared for his first communion (if they even call it that anymore) be a vacuum-brained bimbo with a master's in divinity from a disintegrating theology department who will passive-aggressively force the poor kid to sit through an irrelevant New Age slide show about waterfalls and wheat. On the other hand, he won't be taught that an Accountant God dispenses two kinds of grace, sanctifying and actual; on the other hand, he won't be taught that there is anything called grace at all . . . just "giftedness" and "that special feeling." I'm not entirely convinced that he's better off.

Now I'll be the first to admit it: those who long for the Catholic good old days don't remember how bad they really were. A good cure for such longing is simply to indulge it by attending one of those furtively advertised Traditional Roman Catholic Masses at your local Howard Johnson's. They're usually sponsored by groups with names like The Pope Saint Pius the Ninth Society or the White Warrior's League, and the one that I looked in on recently could have anesthetized a benzadrine-addled Fatima cultist. And it's

Finding Fault

certainly true that that criminally clumsy old time religion of tridentine moral theology manuals designed to navigate a justifiably paranoid sinner through perilous currents of evil frequently invoked unreasonable and child-abusing terror. It occasionally paralyzed sensitive and unimaginative souls, true. It left Catholics United for the Faith in its wake, true. But it also made clear to a little kid that just about everything a person does or thinks or even intends has cosmic consequences. What makes that clear to a kid now? Some frustrated television producer's notion of a folk song? The old Church-as-fortress model produced the Syllabus of Errors, true, but it also underwrote an extremely healthy and now lamentably disappearing suspicion that contemporary cultural assumptions might be all screwed up.

And I don't care what anybody says, such suspicion is sorely needed these days. During a recent debate at Notre Dame, the theologian Daniel Maguire made the amazing suggestion that legalized abortion could not be immoral because so many women worldwide had availed themselves of it. Hans Küng, in a recently published *Commonweal* interview, seems to suggest that nothing very wise or significant was experienced or believed or uttered or thought before 1957. Maybe Cardinal Ratzinger's unique everybody-sit-down-and-shut-up approach to theological matters derives from an understandable longing for the days when Catholics used to paint mustaches on the face of the zeitgeist instead of taking it so seriously . . . the days when it

27

Michael O. Garvey

was taught that there was a great deal more to Christian life than being the kind of character Michael Landon always plays on television.

Regardless of my competence to leave the kid with a bit of this wisdom, there will soon, whether I like it or not, be some M. Div-waving, banana-bread-baking, green-felt-on-burlap-banner-waving, pantheistic director of religious education offering, in the words of the B.B. King song, "some hep I don't need." This DRE (with the arrogance of bureaucrats, they always refer to themselves in initials) will be schooled less in the scholastic irrelevances of Thomist seminary classes and more in the institutionalized vacuities of Southern California self-absorption. You know: Thou shalt not make value judgments; thou shalt shun dichotomies; thou shalt not be negative; thou shalt affirm everything that doesn't make value judgments, etc.

This DRE (I don't even know her name yet, but I already hate her) will read to my kid from texts which seem to have been composed in hammocks by bourgeois geeks toked out on skunkweed. This DRE will mistake hugging for affection, neurosis for guilt, feelings for revelations, "nice" for good. No loony admonitions about impure thoughts, certainly, but no readings from Francis de Sales, either. The vision of the Church (excuse me . . . we're no longer allowed that definite article) the vision *of Church* upheld by this DRE will be vague, uninteresting and unpersuasive. And therefore debilitating.

Finding Fault

It was easy for a conscientious parent to combat the excesses which accompanied that old time religion: When the irascible Monsignor Nameless told our Saint Agnes first grade class that we should be profoundly thankful "because God could have created you all niggers if he'd wanted to," our mother gently suggested that we pray for Monsignor Nameless because he was goofier than a pet racoon. When the stouthearted, and, in fact, stout Sister Infelicitous told our second grade class that God turned his back on us when we sinned, our father indignantly insisted that God would not even turn his back on the sinner as doughbrained as Sister Infelicitous. The heresies in those days were great muscular gorillas of untruth which ran at you roaring and beating their chests, but they weren't . . . well, boring.

These days the heresies come quietly, in greater numbers, and settle around you gradually, like those alien spores in the Invasion of the Body Snatchers, or the Happy Meal iconography of McDonald's hamburgers. For instance, a kid comes home with this weird homework assignment from his religion teacher: "Your name is special, and you are special. Write a list of the special things that your name says about you. How does your name make you special? Draw a design that says what your name says." So much for the opportunity to discuss the lives of the saints. Too negative, or something.

Is this Hallmark Card foolishness really preferable

to those fascinating panegyrics about the chastity of Maria Goretti? It's not only not worth staking your life on, it isn't even very interesting.

A Prophecy in North Little Rock

REV. Pat Robertson was running for president at the time, grinning like Alfred E. Newman on a *Mad Magazine* cover, raving his way through Dixie, discerning Cuban nukes and manfully expressing a Christian solidarity with the spectacularly repentant Rev. Jimmy Swaggart, who had startled his congregation and delighted the couch potatoes of the northern hemisphere by confessing some unsavory carryings on with a Baton Rouge prostitute. Whatever God may have thought of the matter, you just knew that the consequent slump in Jerry Lee Lewis' preaching cousin's ratings was temporary, and that during the next fiscal year he would certainly clear more than the Catholic Church worldwide.

You had to admit it: the stuff in the newspapers and on the airwaves was just *great* for those few weeks, even if there was something boorish and hokey about the actors. But as thoroughly enjoyable and fascinating as these reruns of the Elmer Gantry Show had been, they couldn't distract us discriminating couch potatoes in the Roman Church from the less (far, far less) televisible troubles afflicting our own ministers at the time. True, Jimmy Swaggart and Pat Robertson had tied for first place in the wackadoo contest, but they were not the only North American preachers capable of controversy.

31

Michael O. Garvey

One Sunday morning right around then, for instance, a Mrs. Beulah J. Rupert of Sherwood, Ark., astonished 600 homily-anesthetized parishioners of Immaculate Conception Catholic Church in North Little Rock by bellowing a rebuke at Father Bernard Servil, who had been preaching a sermon which suggested to those awake and listening that our government's support of the Nicaraguan *contras* was immoral. Angrier than an interrupted Pope at a Sandinista seminar, Mrs. Rupert leaped out of her seat, noisily upbraided Father Servil for "bringing up politics" and stormed out of the church carrying six similarly outraged folk in her wake, God bless her.

You had to leave unexamined the compelling evidence that this outburst had erupted from the sort of discontented parishioner who plays the grandkid's rock albums backwards in search of disguised satanic lyrics. After all, every Catholic parish has (and needs) at least three such old ladies. You also had to forget that Father Servil was absolutely correct: United States subsidy of an army distinguished solely by the number of noncombatants it could kill was evil and must end.

Then you could focus on what Henry James would call the "precious particle" of the North Little Rock Embarrassment. A woman had wearied of a homily, had loudly told the offending homilist to fold it four ways and put it where the moon don't shine, and swept out. Exquisite stuff. How could any sensitive, pew-trapped Catholic fail to applaud?

Finding Fault

What sort of sermons were the rest of us passively enduring at precisely the same moment that Beulah Rupert was casting off her shackles? If you go to Mass on Sunday in just about any North American parish, you know. You hear such sermons wherever and whenever the presiding priest has been allowed to forget that inspired speech is not necessarily included in the charisms he received at his ordination. A sample is invariably a condescending mishmash of paraphrase, irrelevance, and anecdote made endurable solely by the knowledge that suffering through it is what one has to do if one wants to receive communion.

Any properly brought up Catholic child learns early on that nothing useful, significant, or even very interesting is said at Mass from the moment the celebrant concludes the reading of the Gospel to the moment we all begin the liturgy of the Eucharist.

There are exceptions, of course, and Mrs. Rupert provided one on that Sunday morning. Oh, I know there are social scientists among us whose computers can vomit volumes of stats on how the victims of Catholic homilies are acquiescent, consenting adults who are enlightened to hear, as I once did, that the Transfiguration might also be described as a "peak experience," or that an episode of the Cosby Show contains some unique message about love and human striving. But an overwhelming 98.2 percent of the North American parishioners I recently surveyed answered "yes" to the question: "Do the homilies you hear weekly make you strongly suspect that a practical

Michael O. Garvey

joke is being played or an anthropological experiment conducted on your parish?" The other 1.8 percent were asleep in the pews around me.

Perhaps it should be noted that Immaculate Conception is the largest Catholic church in Arkansas, a state smack dab in the middle of the Bible Belt, a region where your average product of your average Catholic seminary must compete, as preacher, with your average by-God, bible-bangin', butt kickin', high steppin', mouth foamin', foot stompin', cut-it-all-loose, well—well Jimmy Swaggart-type. If environment can affect anything, your average Arkansas native, regardless of denominational affiliation, comes to church with a significantly weakened resistance to the anemic quality of your average contemporary Catholic sermon.

So it had to occur to you that the six folks who exited Immaculate Conception behind Mrs. Rupert were probably bored to the point of hallucination and desperately searching for an excuse, any excuse, to leave. You had to think of the dozens of Sunday mornings when you would have greedily seized upon such an opportunity to escape. You could only wish that you were as courageous as Beulah Rupert, that you could stand up and confront Sister Mary First Reading and Father Sominex and shout: "Hear me, you pretentious geeks! Your prattling and yammering subjects the very Word of God to the bourgeois flatulence of your enfeebled imaginations. Week after week you require us to sit through your vapid observations before we

Finding Fault

can receive the Eucharist. Our children whine of their boredom and your own less avoidable whining inclines us to confess to them that we, too, are bored. Fall silent, then, or bear on your conscience the loss of these little ones whom we can interest no longer!"

The whole Church on that Sunday had been invited to hear and reflect on a passage in the Gospel according to Mark, describing how a Capernaum synagogue crowd was kept "spellbound" by the note of authority with which our Lord addressed them. Simply put, folks paid attention to this newcomer, because he seemed to have something important to say. Maybe the churchgoers of Capernaum, like those in Little Rock and most of the rest of us, had sat through a few millenia of preaching whose tedium might occasionally become so acute as to awaken them to an agony which they would endure because of convention or even simple politeness. Mark didn't record what Jesus said that day, in fact. The news was that it sounded new.

You teach your kids what your parents taught you: that this side of the Second Coming, access to the newcomer means taking up one's cross, even so light a cross as liturgical boredom. The presence of Christ in the Eucharist doesn't depend on the eloquence of a priest, and even to grumble about these things in that presence seems a sort of blasphemy.

But in the meantime, I hope he forgives me the furtive pleasure I take in knowing that at every Mass there may be a Beulah Rupert seeking whom she may confront.

In Praise of Naval Gazing

KARL MARX was wrong about several things, but especially about religion being the opiate of the people. Politics is.

And if nothing can be done to prevent Catholics from getting zonked in the political opium den, something at least should be done about the opaque language we use to describe our hallucinations. As every issue that comes along becomes an occasion for determining which side everybody's on, everybody should become more precise in expression.

The first thing that should be made clear (or else abolished) is a collection of words such as "ministry" (by which many writers seem to mean anything done by or to Christians which isn't rape), "holistic" (by which seems to be meant "whole"), "authentic" (which has replaced "valid" and seems really to mean "my") and, most obviously, "conservative" and "liberal" (neither of which means anything anymore).

Along with purging our discussions of buzz words and slogans, we should try to be more thorough and honest. If, for instance, we don't see legal abortion as a pressing issue of conscience, we should say something like this: The lives and rights of unborn human beings are less significant than those of born human beings. Christianity does not oblige us to acknowledge that what is done to an unborn human being is done to

36

Finding Fault

Christ. There are more urgent moral concerns in the public order than the millions of legal abortions which have taken and are taking place since abortion became legal.

If we believe in unilateral nuclear disarmament, we must not be content to say (as no less admirable a man than Daniel Berrigan once did), "My problem is that I don't want to kill people," but should say instead something like this: it is true that unilateral disarmament would make us vulnerable to all sorts of horrors (unilateral armament has *already* made us so). We don't know what the response of the "other side(s)" would be. We *do* know that the gospel makes no promises about the national security of the United States of America, and that the way to the Father of Jesus includes the cross.

We may assume that if Our Lord were presented with the choice which now confronts us, the choice of being a victimizer or a victim, he would choose the latter, and we believe there are certain forms of security which faithfulness to Jesus precludes. We don't believe that proponents of the arms race *want* to kill people, but we fear that that is precisely what they are doing, and we cannot be their accomplices.

The world of secular politics is replete with lies and carefully crafted mirages, the work of the wolves among which we, the sheep, must forage. It is the terrain in which Christ told us to be as wise as serpents. But we don't serve him well by *imitating* the serpents. True, we had better pay attention to their political ac-

Michael O. Garvey

tion committees, their lobbying efforts, their image-building and their mastery of the media. But we can't let a fascination with their power and persuasiveness become too strong an invitation. The Book of Genesis is eloquent on that point.

In a colorful letter to his friend Robert Lax, Thomas Merton once wrote that there was "too damn much zowie and bam" in the church's dialogue during the mid-1960s, and said that he wanted "more kiss of God in the mossy wood, more gazing at the navel."

Whether or not we agree with the unofficial doctor of the twentieth-century church, we should at least try to rid our discussions on large social issues of the zowie and bam and fill them instead with the spirit of One who once said, "Plain yes or no is all you need to say; anything beyond that comes from the devil" (Matthew 5:37).

Discussions so undertaken might be occasionally frustrating. We might lose some of the emotive satisfaction which comes along with making our opponents look as ludicrous as we think they should, but we might (even accidentally) shed some light in a region where darkness now reigns. We might also be usefully frightened when we see how far that region extends into our own hearts.

A Pressing Need

A GRUMPY associate once suggested to our Lord
that he might be giving scandal by accept-
ing the lavish gift of a repentant whore, what with
people going starving and all. Luxuries, the associate
thought, should be converted into cash and cash into
food for the empty bellies of the nation's children.
Jesus responded to this complaint with a striking re-
minder that none of his followers would ever have to
look too far to find misery. This, though, seemed a
special case. Awed by the contrast between her interior ugliness and his unfailing welcome, the heart-
broken woman clearly needed to express her gratitude. Her gesture was tacky, true, but loving and
chaste, and he needed to show her that he appreciated
her gift. There would never again be a similar opportunity for her, or for him.

In light of the fact that the grumpy associate later
turned traitor in return for some church petty cash,
hanged himself in a paroxysm of self-loathing, and became memorialized as a paragon of disloyalty, I suppose we should all be a little hesitant to grumble about
the seemingly impetuous expenditures of the kingdom's funds which have occurred since then.

But hey, everybody, we've just dropped 27 million
balloons for a new building in Washington, D.C., in
which to headquarter the National Conference of

Michael O. Garvey

Catholic Bishops. Twenty-seven million. That's enough to physic a Trump.

I know, I know, pastoral letters on public policy don't write themselves and there are 60 million or so Catholic Americans who need to be administered, and conferences to be held and documents to be filed and mailings to be done and secular institutions to be aped and groveled before. These pursuits, as a bus trip through the District of Columbia makes apparent, require large and expensive buildings. Speaking of bus trips, the National Museum Society sponsored a $9 per ticket tour of the new building before the bishops and their staff had unpacked.

Their (or our) old place at 1312 Massachusetts Avenue NW was built during the Second World War when the staff of what was then called the National Catholic Welfare Conference was only a third the size it is now, and I'm willing to take the Church bureaucrats' word that it had become a real dump. And I guess that you do have to have adequate housing for all the administrative machinery necessary to break the hearts of men and women with the relentless mercy of Jesus, to inspire in them the hope of Resurrection, to summon them together in eucharistic community that celebrates God's own presence among them. I suppose it does require thousands of cubic feet of finished office space to startle men and women with the cleavage between their own frailty and mortality and the vastness and immeasurability of the promises of Christ. Perhaps more filing space is needed if our children are to

Finding Fault

be made safe, if the feebleminded, drug-addled, fearful and crazed people wandering our streets (the very streets of Washington, D.C., in fact) are to find welcome in our families and homes.

But 27 million bucks? Was there available nowhere in our land an abandoned Catholic grade school building? How about some of those emptying churches in the slums of Detroit? How about some Catholic university or college willing to chip in a few floors of a building?

Years and years (well, all right, three) ago when the bishops had published their now forgotten pastoral letter on Catholic social teaching and the American economy, I heard Cardinal John O'Connor of New York speak with moving sincerity on an aspect of its provenance. He wondered aloud whether we in the Church were doing anything close to enough for those who starve and watch their children starve, for the terrified single mothers, abused wives and foolish pregnant adolescents so abandoned and despised that they could regard abortion an attractive option. He spoke of the bag ladies and other broken people who roamed the fashionable streets in front of his Manhattan residence, and of the nagging questions their misery presented. He spoke of what he and other bishops had seen when they visited the starving fields of Ethiopia and the Dominican Republic. One of the things he found simultaneously awesome and excruciating was the fact that the enclosure of a simple tent can often spell the difference between life and death for those who suffer both exposure *and* starvation. With what seemed bewilderment, Cardinal O'Connor said over and over, "Fifty dollars. The lack of one of those tents, which costs *fifty dollars*, means that people die." We have to ask ourselves, he said again, not what we have done, but whether we have done enough.

I don't know how the archbishop of New York voted on the matter of the bishops' new national headquarters, but I've wondered since whether such questions as he raised were nagging those bishops in the majority who decided that in the heart of the world's most powerful nation, in the middle of a deranged and voracious society, in a season of global starvation, and in the name of One who came to us in the form of a slave, the kingdom's most pressing need was a $27 million office building.

Another Pressing Need

A CTUALLY, the zorchy new headquarters of the Catholic Church in the United States (where, by the way, are we going to park our hindquarters? Berkeley?) cost 7 million clams more than had been projected. Okay, 6.9 million and some change.

But we've always been sloppy about these matters. When approached by the temple tax collectors at Capernaum, for example, Jesus was exasperated, but told Peter: "Since we don't want to cause offense, go cast a line in the lake, take the first fish that bites, open its mouth and you'll find a silver coin. Take that and pay it in. It will meet the tax for both of us."

Church financial affairs in the subsequent 20 centuries have become even more complicated; Peter's successors have hidden the lake, the line, the hook, the fish, the coin and even the memorandum to Peter. And not so long ago, Catholics learned that the Vatican was $1.27 billion in the hole. It's probably more than that now. All things are possible for God, but where are we going to find a fish with a billion and a half bucks in its mouth? Such a fish would be capable of holding every McDonald's hamburger ever sold with room for those of at least one competing burger chain. Ponder that, ye anglers of Peter's barque.

The central lesson of the Vatican's fiscal blues is simple: the church needs a checking account.

43

Michael O. Garvey

Checking accounts are great. You put in money, write down how much you've put in, add to it the amount that you've already got (or the amount that you've overdrawn) and you can always figure out roughly how much you've got, the fiscal topography of what you can and can't do, and you usually get a number to call when you can't balance the damn thing. Nobody can get mad at you for investing in Krugerands, Marriott Hotels, Coleco toys or questionable money markets.

Fine, you say, but the Church has complicated responsibilities which an individual doesn't: there's *L'Osservatore Romano* to publish, squadrons of Swiss Guards to be paid, nuns, janitors, groundskeepers, and curial paperpushers to pay, to say nothing of papal trips to launch. Fine, I say, then, every year at Peter's Pence time, the Church administrators should publish a budget, explain that there's *L'Osservatore Romano* to publish, squadrons of Swiss Guards to be paid, nuns, janitors, groundskeepers, and curial paperpushers to pay, and papal trips to launch, and ask us to cough up pence appropriately. Most parishes I've been in run that way, and they all seem to be keeping a nostril above water. Why can't the global parish of which we're all members be run the same way?

Another benefit of the Vatican checking account plan is that it would make dust and ashes of that endless debate about whether or not the Church permits usury. Dominican Father Vincent McNabb nicely encapsulated the issue this way:

Finding Fault

To wrest from nature is WORK
To wrest from those who wrest from nature is
TRADE
To wrest from those who wrest from those who
wrest from nature is FINANCE.

Tossing the Peter's Pence collection into a checking account would enable our Church to rest from wresting and to return to the unfinished business of examining gospel poverty which Cardinal Giacomo Lercaro raised and which was tragically plowed under during the Second Vatican Council. There's no getting around that business, after all, and the sooner we all address it, the better.

But the best short term result of a Vatican checking account would be that we wouldn't have to read so much about our Church in the financial section of the newspaper, where we appear too often lately and where, frankly, we don't look so good.

There's a spiritual revolution going on in Russia, the base communities of our Church in Latin America are getting the shaft, a world starved for the truth could still be annihilated by nuclear warfare in a matter of hours, in the industrially developed nations, objecting to the killing of our unborn young is regarded as a radical posture, and southern peoples are as oppressed by northern peoples as ever. In such a world, it is an alarming thought that the community commissioned by Christ to begin building his kingdom can be distracted by a few bouncing checks. A simpler book-

Michael O. Garvey

keeping system might free us to concentrate a little better.

Yet Another Pressing Need

BACK IN 1972, before I had a job, gray hair, kids, sore joints and multiple doubts, one of my favorite professors of theology used a memorable expression to remind those of us who showed up for class that life in the church—life, in other words—could be a complicated and unpredictable affair. "You think you have everything all figured out," he used to say, "and then original sin comes up behind you and bites you on the ass."

I was reminded of his observation recently as I was combing the newspaper in search of unread Reagirantragate material. Predisposed to outrage, and a little disappointed that there were no new Reaganauts twisting slowly, slowly on the spit, I fell eagerly on an item about a new controversy in the ever-controversial world of defense spending. The U.S. Army, according to the article, is blowing 15.6 million smackers on 315,600 new bayonets. That came out to $49.56 apiece.

Think, I thought, of all the finer things you could do with $49.56. Not only minimally decent things such as contributing to alleviate the misery of starving families in Eritrea, or making a gigantic serving of *huevos rancheros* for the local soup kitchen, or paying off a veteran pensioner's electric bill, but also decently lavish things like sending your wife a dozen long-stemmed

Michael O. Garvey

American Beauty roses, or buying your children a crate of rubber lizards, or contracting for a banana cream pie to be thrown at a pompous boss. But $49.56 for a bayonet?

All morality aside, I thought, it's outrageous. Whatever else happens, those poor deranged adolescents who've been taught to be all that they can be will never get within bayonet-charging range of the Nicaraguan farmers and Lebanese Shi'ite toddlers against whom their seniors wish to deploy them. And even if they could, as anyone who has read Eric Maria Remarque's *All Quiet on the Western Front* knows, clubbing is preferred to stabbing by soldiers who survive to describe their closest combats.

The article got worse. The $15.6 million bayonet contract was going to some new southern California company. We all know (at least I do) what sorts of people run and make profit from new southern California companies. Yuppies, flakes, vegetarians, New Age geeks, herbal tea drinkers, sunshine zapoids. A company based in Providence, R.I., that has been manufacturing Uncle Sam's unused bayonets since before the Second World War had put in a lower bid but had, nevertheless, lost the contract. We all know (at least I do) what sorts of people are employed by 70-year-old Providence-based companies. Pleasant Italian grandfathers who look like Pope John XXIII and can't wait for retirement and more time with the grandkids; recently married, industrious Portuguese trying to make a better life for their children; gruffly

Finding Fault

good-natured and paternally complected Irish moon-lighters—the kinds of people you could tranquilly leave your kids with.

Christmas this year would be a gray and cheerless affair for the forlorn children of these wholesome New England households. (Please don't cry, Honey. We lost that bayonet contract and I lost the job, but we still have each other. And we all think you make the best oatmeal in the whole world, don't we, kids? How about a big Christmas hand for Mom?) Meanwhile, those organically sterilized New Age, avocado-brained, family-planning southern Californian pagans would be whetting overpriced knives on some sunny Pacific shore, suddenly able to afford a few more lines of their Bolivian marching powder. Working myself into a pleasantly self-righteous rage, I read on.

And I was, as my theology professor had warned that we all would be, bitten. The new bayonet at the center of this controversy is not, the Army insists, merely a bayonet, but also "a field-craft knife, a combat knife and a wire-cutter," a veritable "multipurpose instrument." The phrase arrested me, and I was booked on a charge of obsession with intent to possess a gadget. And guilty as charged.

People in my family have always had a weakness for gadgets. In one of my earliest memories, I'm sitting on my grandfather's lap and he's delighting me with his watchfob, a gleaming, stainless steel bauble designed to clip holes in cigars. And Grandpa didn't even smoke. My mother uses an electric device that doubles

Michael O. Garvey

as a can opener and orange-juicer; my father haunts the remotest areas of his house and yard waiting for incoming calls on a cordless and portable telephone; my youngest boy wants nothing so much as a Swiss Army knife; and now I find myself in dire need of this newfangled bayonet, which, according to the newspaper account, "can snip double-twisted barbed wire, cut half-inch hemp rope, slice metal bands on ammunition carriers and saw aircraft fuselages." It didn't say whether the bayonet had a compass embedded in its handle, but I'll bet it does. It also has a shiny finish on the blade (which, of course, means that you can flash secret code signals on sunny days and use it as a rudimentary mirror when you're miles away from the nearest bathroom.)

With such an implement, I could do just about anything and go just about anywhere, and my previously incoherent life would finally be made whole again. I could subdue the lilacs in our backyard and clip away the rusted barbed wire of the derelict fence along the alley. I could become undisputed master of our garage and basement. I could carry it in the glove compartment when we went on long car trips, confident as the Swiss family Robinson. I would take the family out camping for weeks in the woods with no more than this bayonet and our sacred bonds. I could open letters and cans of tuna fish with it, to say nothing of what I could do to the tomcat two doors down, the one that insists upon spraying the side of our house and defecating in our sandbox.

Finding Fault

My newly discovered need of the silliest and most outdated item of the NATO arsenal is sufficiently wholesome to be disquieting. I don't apologize for it, but I can't help but wonder whether it rests on a continuum with our collective and national "need" for some of the flashier and more genocidal items on the Pentagon wish list. An Air Force pilot friend once rapturously described the exhilaration of flying a fighter jet (an F-something or other) upside-down and perilously close to the surface of the Atlantic, zooming along a solid and ice-blue ceiling at I-can't-remember-how-many-miles-an-hour. For a moment we both forgot what fighter jets are designed to do. A man who refuses to see how much fun that stunt would be has put to death the child in himself. And a man sufficiently trained to pull off such a stunt must also be ready to put to death children for reasons of state.

Such things should come to mind when we set out to judge the mad technicians of "national security," "effective law enforcement" and "reproductive freedom." Their fantasies loom in our children's future like the gates of some imminent Auschwitz, true, but their fantasies are also our own—grounded in an ingenious, stricken and sickened imagination we all share with our victims and tormentors. It's a disturbing article of our faith that the human imagination can be made whole and harmonious only when we acknowledge its depravity and beg God's mercy for it.

Answering an Inconvenient Question

ONE fall day not so long ago, Pope John Paul II
had twenty-three American bishops out to his
place in Castelgondolfo for a visit, and much of what
he said to them and a little of what they said to him
made it into our newspapers. At least to this lazy
reader, most of what he said to them seemed to be the
stuff that you'd expect a Pope to say; stuff that bishops
need to remind each other of from time to time: that a
bishop's compassion is ill-expressed when it bashfully
avoids hard sayings; that what the Church teaches is
not mere human wisdom; that revealed truth isn't always immediately palatable; that shepherding souls
isn't always a day at the beach. These are admonitions
which might be equally useful to all the baptized,
whose complicated and often daunting responsibility
it is to look to their bishops for a sign of unity, who
must, whether they like it or not, attempt to see Christ
in their bishops as well as in each other.

But the Holy Father could do a bit more to enhance
the view.

I think about the ordination of women as frequently
as I think about the ordination of men—which is to
say about once every two months, usually after a particularly unpleasant encounter with a recipient of
Holy Orders. People who feel strongly about the issue

52

Finding Fault

(on both sides) are usually bores about it, and I pray that if any future pope does decide that women should no longer be excluded from the sacrament of Holy Orders, he'll follow the wise suggestion to reject the first 4000 applicants. Either that, or put them to work in Rome.

But if I *did* feel strongly about the issue, I don't think I would care to have my enthusiasm lumped together (as it increasingly seems to be in Rome) with lax attitudes about sexual promiscuity and adultery and the killing of the unborn. There are, after all, people who love the Church no less than does Pope John Paul II, who *because* they love the Church (and not because feminism is trendy) believe that the exclusion of females from the priesthood is scandalous.

Some of these people believe, rightly or wrongly, that papal insistence upon a monosexual and celibate priestly ministry is grounded in and generates a weird scale of values in which access to the Eucharist is presented as less urgent than a badly explained sexual rectitude. Most people, at any rate, acknowledge that it is at best embarrassing to have such an odd insistence held up for all the world to see.

To be sure, none of us has been baptized to avoid embarrassment, and there are other insistences in our tradition which appear nutty to the world. Our assertion that men and women who marry must live together for life and must want and welcome children and open their homes to strangers doesn't seem compatible with most contemporary ways of making do, but it can be compellingly explained to anyone who believes that Jesus is Lord.

And it's possible, just possible, that the women-need-not-apply approach to the priesthood might be similarly explained. But it hasn't been, and I'm beginning to wonder if it can be.

It might well be that when our Lord decided to invite all human beings to a banquet for which he would be host, food, and fellow guest, he thought it best that women sit quietly at the table. It might well be that when he said, "Do this in memory of me," his command was addressed solely to celibate males. It might well be that those whose attention fastens more on *what* Christ says to do than on *who* should or should not do it, that such people, as the Pope said to the bishops "are in fact damaging the very dignity of women that they profess to promote and advance." But if the many proponents of women's ordination are as dangerously out to lunch as John Paul says they are, the serious and not yet undertaken task before the Holy Father is to explain where they've gone wrong.

A good bishop, the Pope said to his American brothers, must "endeavor to explain as cogently as he can that the Church's teaching on the exclusion of women from priestly ministry is extraneous to the issue of discrimination and that it is linked rather to Christ's own design for his priesthood." That sounds to me as if the Pope was saying that a good bishop is obligated to do something which nobody has yet done

Finding Fault

and which the Bishop of Rome has so far failed to do. Which doesn't seem exactly fair.

When John Paul's predecessor of happy memory opened his first session of the Second Vatican Council, he said, "Nowadays, the Spouse of Christ prefers to make use of the medicine of mercy rather than that of severity. She considers that she meets the needs of the present day by demonstrating the validity of her teachings rather than by condemnations." But it is difficult to avoid the suspicion that Pope John Paul does not feel compelled to meet advocates of women's ordination with a demonstration of anything other than his displeasure.

Don't get me wrong. For all I know, his displeasure is fully justified. "Shut up," he explained, is one always available response to an inconvenient question. But it's a hell of a way to run a Church.

Ratzinger as Art Critic

A JOKE recently making the rounds in these parts goes like this:

Charles Curran, Hans Küng and Joseph Ratzinger all died on the same day. On their approach to the celestial turnstile, they met, as we all eventually must, St. Peter. "Three celebrities at once!" exclaimed the keeper of the keys. "I think I'd better arrange personal interviews for all of you." They were called in alphabetical order to meet face-to-face with the Boss. Charles Curran, shaken but overjoyed, emerged from the office of God the Father after 15 minutes. Peter, Hans and Joseph, loitering in the lobby, all looked up from their magazines. "I didn't do as badly as I thought," said Charlie. "Only 15 years in purgatory!" After the Catholic University professor had left to begin his sentence, Hans Küng went inside. This time, the door was closed for a full hour. Hans came out trembling, but greatly relieved. "He is merciful indeed," Hans said to Peter and Joseph. "After a mere century of purgative exile, I will again be allowed to gaze on his face." It was Joseph's turn now to meet his judge. He remained inside for five minutes, after which God the Father Almighty emerged from his office and said to Peter, "That wasn't so bad. His Eminence is letting me off with only 20 years in purgatory."

The joke, of course, is a bit impolite to the prefect of

Finding Fault

the Congregation for the Doctrine of the Faith. But then, why be polite to the Congregation for the Doctrine of the Faith? After all, he heads a crucial office in an institution that St. Francis de Sales has described metaphorically as an ignoble beast of burden carrying the treasure of the true faith. Which means that it may be said with scrupulous accuracy, fraternal respect and loyal affection that his eminence Cardinal Joseph Ratzinger is a pain in the ass.

I'll admit that this attitude is ungrateful. After all, as one of the ordinary faithful, I enjoy the doctrinal protection of the Holy Office's regular theological inoculations. It has provided me a perfectly respectable excuse (orthodoxy) for not reading whatever it was that Curran so irreverently published about masturbation back in the 1960s. After all, a theologian who can read or write or speak about (or perhaps even accomplish) masturbation without so much as a giggle is clearly not very helpful and probably not very wise.

Ratzinger has also exempted me from the still-unfinished task of reading Hans Küng's *On Being a Christian.* A friend of mine, a notorious but very capable liar, once convinced me that he'd read that book and that I should, too. Ingenuously, I went at the monster full tilt, page after page after unimaginable tedious page, discovering the truth of Logan Pearsall Smith's observation that boredom can become almost a mystical experience. By page 175 or so, a few lifetimes later, Küng's cloudy prose had me on a backslapping, first-name basis with everyone in the Blessed Trinity.

Michael O. Garvey

Now I'm absolutely certain that *nobody*, not Ratzinger, not Curran, not even those passionate academics who claim solidarity with whatever it is that Küng is getting at, has really read *On Being a Christian*. But Ratzinger has given all of us who will admit that we haven't read it an even better reason than the book's remarkable capacity to grow unread pages even as you read: orthodoxy.

His eminence the zinger of rats, our lugubrious Brother Joseph, has been very kind to us Mass-going, envelope-using, bulletin-reading, kid-raising, priest-ridden, bishop-afflicted, pope-forsaken laity. He has defended us from the wickedness and snares of theology, even from theology itself. So why kick him around in our grumbling small talk? I'll tell you why: The man is a humorless old twit, a Bavarian beanbag, a sourpuss extraordinaire, a curmudgeon's curmudgeon, a pickle-weaned prince of the church. It makes perfect sense that the most popular photo of Ratzinger has him sitting in front of a painting of some beheaded unfortunate.

Not to put too fine a point on it: He don't dig rock 'n' roll music.

Did I say he don't *dig* rock 'n' roll? He *loathes* the stuff. Says it's "the complete antithesis of Christian faith in the redemption." Hearken, you who know the real lyrics of "Louie, Louie," to his recent utterance of his Teutonic Tunedeafness as quoted in our diocesan weekly. You can almost hear the pursing of the guy's lips: "In a way which we could not imagine 30 years

58

Finding Fault

ago, music has become the decisive vehicle of a counterreligion and thus calls for a parting of the ways. Since rock music seeks release through liberation from the personality and its responsibility (say *what?*), it can be on the one hand precisely classified among the anarchic ideas of freedom which today predominate more openly in the West than in the East. But that is precisely why rock music is so completely antithetical to the Christian concept of redemption and freedom, indeed its exact opposite." Gotcha, Eminence. So you'd put, say, Lawrence Welk right about in the mainstream of orthodoxy. Thanks for sharing that with us.

Joseph Ratzinger's rather embarrassing emergence as an authority on rock music makes me wonder whether he could sing you so much as a single stanza of "Wake Up Little Suzie," or name three songs by Fats Domino, or come within a decade of naming the dates of The Grateful Dead's famous European tour. And if this noninfallible teaching is something from which we may dissent. And if his Eminence isn't a little, you know—funny.

Holding A Self Like Water

AN OLD friend of mine, a priest, has withdrawn his vow of celibacy. He loves and intends to marry another friend, a woman who also loves him. Both are good people, and I wish them immeasurable joy. Perhaps I shouldn't find the news of his decision and departure so distressing.

I can't give a very eloquent defense of the institutional arrangements which have for years separated my two friends from a peaceful marriage bed, because I think those arrangements are foolish. I believe that Rome's insistence upon celibacy as a prerequisite for ordination to the priesthood will eventually go the way of Tridentine Mass, and God speed the day. Unlike the Tridentine Mass, it won't be much of a loss.

Don't get me wrong: I'm not down on celibacy. Ours is a pretty ruttish society after all. The advertising firms responsible for our imaginations insist on letting copulation thrive, no matter how frivolous, exploitative or lethal. In that mass market which is our culture's real religion there are no problems, only opportunities, and even something as horrifying as an AIDS epidemic serves largely as a way to stimulate the condom market and fill the airwaves with platitudes about "safe" and (I didn't make this up) "compassionate" sex. Not even lust can any longer escape the expert tyranny and fine tuning of public relations.

Finding Fault

Now more than ever, the Catholic Church seems to be the best friend sex ever had. Now more than ever, the grace of celibacy ought to be celebrated and revered. But that is not necessarily what happens when celibacy is required of a priest.

I've been fortunate (perhaps I should say blessed) enough to have met men and women—more often than not in monasteries, but in some other forms of religious community as well—in whom celibacy seems a strength and a gift; an indication of a ferocious mystery; a witness to the unimaginable meeting with the Father of Jesus which is our ultimate vocation.

Still, there seems to me more aversion to sex and intimacy than devotion to Gospel and Kingdom in the confusing association our Church maintains of celibacy with *priesthood*. Without claiming expertise in these things, I can honestly say that the diocesan priests I have met in my lifetime have, nearly to a man, expressed celibacy as strange, exhausting, destructive and tragic. Appearances often deceive, but very few of these have seemed to be happy or even healthy men. They have often seemed strikingly asexual or disconcertingly effeminate; they have often displayed an alarming reliance on drink, drug, latenight television and/or a juvenile kind of consumerism. While I hope I have tried hard enough to love, respect and pray for them and while I know I have gratefully accepted their service, it has always been difficult for me to understand how our Church is served by their pathologies. According to our folklore, celibacy frees a diocesan

Michael O. Garvey

priest for an otherwise impossibly singlehearted devotion to the Church's members, but I was raised in a warm and close family whose parents always seemed as passionately and perpetually available to those in need as any priest I know. They believed, and taught their children to believe, that Baptism, not Holy Orders, calls each of us to an unreasonable availability.

I have a hunch that purposely celibate men living outside close, faithful, and perhaps even monastic communities, become less praiseworthy than weird. It seems to me that our hierarchy's nonchalance about this renders far too many already troubled men even weirder, inflicting the embittered, often dangerous, and invariably burdensome results on the Catholic children, couples, families and communities who have no other obvious access to the Eucharist. Our harried bishops seem insensitive to this misfortune. They, unlike harried layfolk, have no ingenuous children for whom they must charitably interpret the shakey demeanor of a broken man who presides at Eucharist. To demand that every priest exemplify the integrity to which each of us is summoned may be asking too much, but to require of every priest at least as much maturity and balance as a responsible parent would require of an adolescent babysitter seems reasonable enough. At any rate, those who condone current Church usage of celibacy really shouldn't complain about the current profusion of weak and inadequate priests the Church suffers. It is troubling that the celibate vow is required of those to whom we confess our

Finding Fault

sins and around whom we gather when we celebrate Mass. It is troubling that the deterioration of an anti-social young man attracted by a comfortable regimen, an odd wardrobe and isolation from women can be disguised by the vow. It is troubling that the persistent refusal to ordain those who have not taken the vow, even in priestless regions fertile with belief, sends a confusing—no, really blasphemous—message about the importance of the Eucharist.

But it is every bit as troubling that we've become people so adept at releasing ourselves and each other from this or any vow which constrains our wills. We have become so numb to God and ourselves and each other that even our most sacred promises exert no very strong claim on us. One of the best, if most sobering gifts I've ever heard of was given by a woman I know to her husband on the morning of their wedding. A framed beautiful piece of calligraphy which still hangs in their bedroom it is a quote from a memorable scene in Robert Bolt's play about Thomas More, *A Man For All Seasons*. More is imprisoned in the Tower of London. His daughter, Margaret, is begging him to yield to the King, swear to the Act of Succession, and return home. More replies: *"When a man takes an oath, Meg, he's holding his own self in his own hands. Like water. And if he opens his fingers then—he needn't hope to find himself again. Some men aren't capable of this, but I'd be loathe to think your father one of them."* Oaths, vows, all those carefully chosen words we say to God, are scary things. It is awesome

Michael O. Garvey

to speak them and almost equally so to hear them spoken. We ought to approach them warily and we ought to be uneasy when they are withdrawn. But we don't and we aren't. It's been said that secularism is a lie about reality: We've become increasingly secular.

In the Church, those apparently impossible things we demand of our members—that our spouses remain unconditionally faithful to each other until death; that those of us who forego the servitude of marriage fast from its deepest joy as well; that those of us who seek the special grace of a special community place their entire persons at its service—are ways we defy the suffocating logic of the world. Distracted as we may be by the world's quite reasonable claims of power, appetite, convenience and necessity, we make a point of rejecting them all, and insist that Our Lord's quite *un*reasonable claims alone will make a man out of a man and a woman out of a woman. At times these claims seem to be ripping us apart, and to the extent that we rely on our own strength, they probably are. At times this counterculture seems to oppose simply human desire, and to the extent that such desire is too feeble, it probably does. At times this cross seems to be killing us, and to the extent that we cling to our old selves, it probably is. The kingdom of God isn't cheap.

In an excellent book entitled *For Better Or Worse: Sober Thoughts on Passionate Promises* (Paulist Press $5.95) James Tunstead Burtchaell has this to say about the witness of Catholic marriage in an age when its

Finding Fault

pledge of mutual unconditional lifelong fidelity seems bizarre: *At this time of epidemic divorce, of the scorning of marriage and the abandonment of children, of disbelief in fidelity to pledges or in devotion stubborn enough to yield joy—precisely at this time we should shout that the way of marriage is the way of survival, that the most certain thing we know is to undertake what is least certain, that tenacity until death defies and defeats death. It is the look in the eyes of Jesus crucified.* What Burtchaell writes about marriage surely holds true for other sacred vows, including that of celibacy, as well.

I have too many good friends in heartbreaking torment, friends who find themselves lonely and unhappily celibate, who chafe and choke in difficult marriages, who are homosexual and in profound anguish, who groan in obedience to fatuous superiors, who are stifling in immature communities. All of these people have made solemn promises in better times, and the individuals and families and communities to whom they have sworn lifelong service have changed, often in unimaginably dreadful ways. I wish I could convince myself that their vows didn't mean what they said. I wish I believed that they hadn't pledged themselves utterly to a service which they now find too taxing to continue. But when they hedge, even a friend, no, especially a friend, can't help but mourn the failure. How can I celebrate their choices when their choices strain and weaken that whole fabric of unstinting, life-

Michael O. Garvey

long promises, a fabric into which my own marriage vow is woven, the very "stuff" of our Church clumsily bearing witness to the power of our risen Lord?

I have no right to judge. As a spoiled son of that Church, a faltering disciple halfheartedly faithful in the easiest of times, I'm accustomed to flee from any cross, large or small. I'd like to be able to tell my friends that I see nothing shameful in their doing likewise. I'd like to be able to tell them that their own flight is a matter of indifference to me, a matter of indifference, period. It's not. I can't. God have mercy on us all.

Updating Opus Dei's Penance Rites

IT WAS a cold northern Indiana night. We'd said night prayers with the kids and tucked them in, and I'd just finished kicking my wife around the living room while she said the Memorare. I was beginning the Salve Regina and she was uncoiling our favorite bullwhip when I was distracted by the memory of something I'd read in the *New York Times* a few days before.

Monsignor Alvaro del Portillo y Diez de Sollano, the Opus Dei boss, had dismissed an interviewer's questions about Opus Dei's encouragement of self-flagellation with the remark, "It's not such a terrible thing. . . . I laugh when I read about it—it is so little. It is much worse what the husband does to the wife, and the wife to the husband."

"Don't scream so loudly, Dear. You'll wake the children," my wife said, between lashes.

"I was just thinking aloud, Love. Sorry."

"I couldn't hear you over the whipcracking, Darling. Let me get the rubber hose. It's quieter. Now then," she said, between thumps, "you were thinking?"

"About that Opus Dei thing in the *Times*. What that Monsignor Whoosit said."

"I'm sorry, Honey. We lent the chains to the Moriartys for their anniversary. There's still some barbed wire in the kitchen, though."

"No, Peach. The part about how he feels what Opus Dei does is so little. (Could you do my shoulders some more?) You know, how the hair shirts and flagella don't even approach what married folks can do to mortify the flesh."

"Do you think that's what he meant, Sugar?" Her arm was tired, so we took a break and had a cigarette.

"You have to read between the lines," I said. "Opus Dei's part of the post-Vatican II Church. The man is begging for the insights of lay folk. You know, for our unique experiences and ways that they could be incorporated into Opus Dei spirituality. Don't you think?"

She began to bathe the gashes in my back with iodine. "Could be, Cupcake, but what unique experiences do we married people have that Monsignor What's-His-Name hasn't probably already used to mortify himself?" She saw my grin and blushed. "No, you beast! You couldn't mean . . ."

"But I do, my sweet. We have children!"

So here is our program of mortification: whenever the penitent retires to a quiet place to pray, a child accompanies him; whenever the penitent retires to a quiet place to sleep, ditto. When the penitent awakens to say his morning offering, a child is present, asking for Cheerios; when the penitent gets Cheerios for the child, the child informs him that there is no milk; when the penitent gets milk, the child demands more sugar; the penitent informs the child that there is already too

Finding Fault

much sugar on the Cheerios and that too much sugar is not good for a child.

The child has a tantrum. The penitent tries to escape to the bathroom—forget the morning offering. The penitent wants the quiet, or a false consolation, if you will. The child bangs on the door of the bathroom; the child has forgotten the sugar on the Cheerios and wants to watch "Sesame Street."

The penitent bolts from the bathroom and falls on the television set like a drowning man on driftwood. "Mr. Rogers" is on, but the child wants to see "Sesame Street." The penitent remembers that "Sesame Street" has been canceled and tries, in a quavering voice, to convince the child that "Mr. Rogers" is going to disembowel Oscar the Grouch today or something; the child is placated until another child, having heard Oscar the Grouch mentioned, wants to see "Sesame Street."

The penitent retreats to the kitchen and the children follow, screaming something about Cheerio Street or Oscar the Milk. When the penitent's wife awakens and wants to know what all the commotion is about, the penitent roars something about disemboweling Mr. Rogers and is driven out into the cold, workaday world to influence its various institutions with his spirituality. It is 8:15 a.m. The penitent has been conscious for one hour and is already wondering, if he's sufficiently recollected to wonder anything, whether it is reprehensibly unorthodox to long for a nice, quiet place in which to beat himself up in peace and quiet.

The only problem with our program of mortification is that if word got back to the Vatican (as it surely would, now that Opus Dei has become a personal prelature) that the society was requiring this discipline of its members—well, you can imagine the scandal.

Standing Against Fuzzyism

T HERE'S simply no hope.
Someone for whose honesty I can vouch was
recently interviewing applicants for a middle-manage-
ment public relations position. Having asked one of
them some standard hypothetical question about
proper administrative dealings with personnel, he
swears he received this response: "Well, I think
everyone needs a pat on the back now and then. In the
Catholic Church, we call it a warm fuzzy."

Wrong. In the Catholic Church, we vomit on that
man's glossary.

Hearing that story, I thought how inadequate our
English language sometimes is. There should be a
word to denote the simultaneously occurring emo-
tions of hilarity, awe, delight and outrage. How do
you share a planet with someone who believes that
warm fuzzies are gifts of the church?

You instruct *him*, fine. How do you share a planet
with someone who *teaches* others that warm fuzzies
are anything more than warm and fuzzy? Worse, who
teaches that warm fuzzies have anything, anything at
all, to do with the triune God or the word made flesh?
"How do you even make fun of these folks?" I groaned
to my father, who had just assured me of the existence
of a theological journal that features a column attrib-
uted to its editor's puppy. "You can't," replied my fa-

Michael O. Garvey

vorite venerable observer of Catholic flakery. "They have a sort of spiritual AIDS. There's simply nothing that can be done for them." I'm afraid he's right. It's easy to forget that the victims of the most rapacious folly are always the folks most immune to humor. Can nothing be done to protect the rest of us (and our children—don't forget that fuzzyists are often attracted to Catholic elementary schools) from them?

Mind you, I'm not advocating a return to the Church of the churching of women, the starching of wimples and the syllabusing of errors. People who get nostalgic for the pre-1960s Church somnolent either can't remember the old girl or are more interested in her funkiness than in her truth. By the end of the current pontificate, in fact, we'll all be so tired of those restored good old days that we'll probably be assiduously futuring our heads off. But in the meantime, something simply must be done to keep the heresy of warm fuzzyism at bay.

The fuzzyists have a stranglehold on (if not a laughing-gas mask over) most Catholic parochial institutions. Lasso 10 directors of religious education, and you'll have custody of at least four folks who will tell you, without embarrassment, that they're "processing" (not thinking, worrying or praying about) some damned thing or other. Approach a dozen parish priests requesting baptism for your child, and nine will hand you over to a barely trainable airhead with a master's in divinity who will require your attendance at a week's worth of evening slide shows about water-

Finding Fault

falls and wheat. I'm not entirely sure this is an improvement over a few passages from Baltimore Catechism No. 12 barked at you by the mildly stoned Monsignor O'Dollar.

To suggest a corrective pastoral letter (titled, say, "North American Bourgeois Self-Absorption and the Integrity of the Church") would be tempting if it weren't so clear that some of the warmest of all possible fuzzyists are openly aided and abetted by fellow travelers (or should they be called fellow sojourners?) in the National Conference of Catholic Bishops. And can you imagine *that* consultation process? Every English-speaking geekbomb of Christendom, every clown minister (Where are the pure, funny, disinterested *clowns* of yesteryear? Dead, now, or ministering, every damn one.), every last goofmonger from every last body prayer workshop, every holistic wackadoo who ever parked buns on a prayer bench would show up demanding a positive episcopal stroke.

But we must do *something* if we and our families are to avoid being cuddled to death by herds of magical mystery bears, sucked under an onrushing tidal wave of smiley faces, shot down in the relentless hail of middle-class spiritual popcorn. One thing to be said in favor of the good old days is that the demons then were at least recognizably fierce and frightening. Their contemporary camouflage is subtly fatuous and flabby. You could drive off those lupine, scary, pre-1960s demons by prayer and fasting, but Snoopy's agents

73

Michael O. Garvey

stalk even the church's holiest precincts today seeking whom they may, well, enable.

Theologians (or, more precisely, published writers with academic degrees in theology) roam unchallenged by their local ordinaries (unchallenged even by ordinary locals) using phrases like "enigmatic constitutedness"; church leaders unabashedly confess membership in a group (I'm not making this up) called "Joygerms International," which espouses hugging as a means of putting people in touch with, well, their huggability, or something.

Not only is all of this saccharine nonsense not worth dying for, not only is it far too masturbatory and self-pitying to base a life or a marriage or a family on, not only does it incorporate the shallowest values of a culture that was already heading down the tubes anyway —but this theological fluff is finally not very interesting (except for those times, as with the theological dog column, when it is bizarre). A person who would be drawn into the church because of it needs an imagination overhaul.

But warm fuzzyism is here for a long while, whether we like it or not, and something has to be done about it.

Catholic Dissent and Sturgeon's Law

A COUPLE of summers ago, it became utterly impossible for any newspaper reader or even television viewer to avoid frequent and regular illustrations of Sturgeon's Law, the principle enunciated by the great science fiction writer (Theodore) that ninety percent of everything is crap.

The most obvious of these was the network coverage of the Democratic and Republican conventions, the controversy arising from the release of what would otherwise be remembered as Martin Scorcese's dumbest film, *The Last Temptation of Christ*, and the furor stirred by the nocturnal illumination of Wrigley Field.

Closer to home, for us Catholics at least, was the departure of Sisters Barbara Ferraro and Patricia Hussey from their religious order, the Sisters of Notre Dame de Namur. The two women, along with dozens of other mostly white, mostly upper-middle class, mostly college-educated, mostly privileged Catholic people had signed a confusingly worded and now famous advertisement which ran in the October 7, 1984, edition of the *New York Times.* Reacting to what they called "continued confusion and polarization within the Catholic community" the signers of the advertisement seldom approached precision but seemed to be saying that there is nothing intrinsically repugnant to the teachings of Jesus in a parent's decision to destroy un-

75

Michael O. Garvey

desired offspring. The advertisement was successful in generating a lively debate, dismaying many of its signers' friends, and annoying high Vatican officials. The more imaginative folks among its signers reaped much publicity and little else.

To my knowledge, none of the signers has so far been excommunicated, arrested, tortured, exiled or executed. I do remember calling up one signer, a friend, and asking her how in the world she could have been persuaded to sign such a silly document, and we argued about it. I assumed, correctly in her case, that by affixing her signature to a public statement, she was proclaiming her willingness to test its validity in fair-minded argument. She was, we have agreed to disagree profoundly, and we're still, I'm happy to say, friends. In similar spirit, the leadership of the Sisters of Notre Dame de Namur very sensibly refused to dismiss Barbara Ferraro and Patricia Hussey and very charitably expressed hope that all concerned—Barbara, Patricia and their religious family—could retrieve their precious and threatened sisterhood with one another.

Then, suddenly one July day, citing "the violence used with us by the leadership" Barbara Ferraro and Patricia Hussey announced their decision to quit. *Violence?* Granting that access to the media requires at least some hyperbole, the grisliness of the issue which had separated these women from their community made their usage all the more arresting. In a *New York Times* article on their leavetaking, Frances Kissling,

Finding Fault

the director of Catholics For a Free Choice emphasized the depth of the tragedy: "You can't know what it's like to sit in the Mother Superior's office and be treated like a bad little girl." But I most certainly could. And it seemed to me that if you were a big girl, you might think Mother Superior's treatment unfair or silly, but you'd square your shoulders, take a deep breath, get on with your work and quit whining about it. All part of becoming a grownup.

Further illustrations of Sturgeon's Law appeared in the ensuing reaction stories. From Ms. Kissling: "Whenever you have Rome cracking down, people are less inclined to take risks." *Risks?* If Ms. Kissling regarded the signing of a *New York Times* ad a risk, her life must have been frought with the most intense and terrifying decisions. Imagine such a sensibility confronted with the drama of a supermarket, steadily approaching the cantaloupes and seizing one to the exclusion of all others. Here I stand, I can do no other.

No: A risk is what Thomas More took when he disobeyed King Henry VIII. A risk is what Joan Andrews took when she unplugged a suction machine in an abortion clinic. A risk is what Franz Jagerstatter took when he refused military service in Austria. A risk is what the brothers Berrigan and their friends took at the draft board office in Catonsville.

From Rev. Charles Curran: "We are existing in a tension-filled atmosphere and Rome is cracking down all over." *Tension-filled? Cracking down?* Oh, come on. The sound of jackboots on the cobblestones wasn't

Michael O. Garvey

exactly deafening those days. Tension-filled might be the bridge of the USS Vincennes as a frightening radar blip approached; tension-filled was the atmosphere on the bridge in Selma as unarmed demonstrators approached furious Alabama state troopers. Tension-filled would be the close air in a carload of Salvadoran catechists at an army roadblock. Tension-filled could hardly be the relatively minor challenge of choosing which talk show appearance to make, which job offer to take and which publishing company to go with. Tension-filled couldn't possibly be the office of some disapproving Mother or Father Superior. Tension-filled wouldn't be some terrible showdown in a Vatican office with a mild-mannered Bavarian clerk. Dissent from official Church teaching may be inevitable, may even be salutary from time to time, but these days it really doesn't cost the dissenter much more than a job change.

Shortly after the "general government group" of the Sisters of Notre Dame de Namur announced its decision to end the dismissal procedings, Srs. Barbara and Patricia convened a press conference which Mr. Sturgeon should have attended. They applauded their community "for not participating in the horizontal violence begun by the hierarchy's intervention in our lives four years ago. Our leadership has shown courage in the face of increased oppression by the Vatican." They pluckily denounced "conformity to church teachings brought about by fear, coercion and threats" and they repeated their conviction that "we

Finding Fault

are not meant to be Eichmann Christians and blindly obedient." Whatever one may think of Vatican fatuity, it's clear that these are women with a pretty low threshold of menace.

Whether or not one agrees with the current crop of Catholic dissenters, it's annoying to hear fine words like "courage" invoked in disputes which seldom have much more than salaries, tenure, or institutional status at their base.

Take a random sample of recently famous dissenters: Hans Küng, Charles Curran, Agnes Mansour, Srs. Barbara and Patricia, and Marcel Lefebvre. Whatever the merits of their various arguments with Rome, if they may be said to have anything in common, it is that none of them, at least in public dealings with curial officials and ecclesial bureaucrats, has ever suffered anything like real violence, needed anything like real bravery, or incurred anything like a true risk.

Either that or each of them is far too frail to be let outdoors without a keeper.

Semper Fi

THERE'S boundless theft in limited professions, so when you hear that clerics, soldiers and congressfolk are meeting and arguing about money it's wise to pay careful attention. That's what was going on a few falls ago in the military church or the ecclesial army or whatever you want to call that confusing realm of the military chaplaincy, where sacraments become Pentagon requisition items and priests receive money, rank and prestige from our nation's armed services in return for extending the ministry of our Church to select government employees.

The problem is that when you are a priest employed by an institution other than the Church, whether that institution be army, whorehouse or university, you have a peculiar frailty in common with the soldier, the prostitute and the professional scholar. You can be fired, even if you, like Admiral John O'Connor, are cardinal archbishop of New York. Or your employer can decide not to hire so many of you. From time to time, even the Pentagon decides to cut back.

And when it does, you can always bitch about it. Which is what inspired a few Catholic priests who came to believe that they were being denominationally underrepresented chaplaincywise (Pentagonspeak seems apposite here) to make some noise.

According to a remarkably ecumenical sort of mili-

Finding Fault

tary minister's lobbying group called the Chaplain's Research Committee, Uncle Sam had failed to open his war chest wide enough for Catholic, Orthodox and Jewish chaplains. A Democratic congressman from Pennsylvania, Robert Borski, agreeing with them, introduced legislation which would require that strikingly pastoral gentleman, Secretary of Defense Weinberger, to rectify the situation by requisition or confiscation of more priests and rabbis, regardless of the fact that this was the one aspect of the arms race in which everybody agreed we were way ahead of the Soviets.

But according to Father George M. Rinkowski, national chaplain, and William Gill, executive director of the Catholic War Veterans of the United States, the complaints of the Chaplains Research Committee and Congressman Borski's proposed legislation were both hypocritical. Executive director Gill said of Father Joseph Turner, the ex-chaplain who directed the Committee, "He's all wet on this. It's his frustration because he got booted out of the Army. That's all it is." National chaplain Rinkowski was more irenic, acknowledging that there was a shortage of Catholic chaplains, but insisting that "our bishops have been doing everything possible." Chaplain Rinkowski added that the Borski proposal would be "foolish legislation. It puts the emphasis on the wrong thing."

Well, he had that last part right anyway. The thing this proposed legislation emphasized was a guarantee that deputies of the Lord got their own piece of an ap-

Michael O. Garvey

parently inexhaustible Pentagon pie, and that was decidedly wrong. But nobody seemed to be talking about how wrong.

And our bishops were certainly not, as Chaplain Rinkowski said, doing everything possible about the problem. In fact, they weren't doing jack squat about the chaplain shortage, and why should they? Chaplains work less for the Church than for the State, and the State should be responsible for them as it is for its other employees. Emphasis had been put on the wrong thing long before the Chaplains Research Committee began its fundraising campaign.

What makes the military chaplaincy possible is the cooperation of churchmen who, having become reprehensibly good American citizens, have learned to see the Church as one more American institution, like the Chrysler Corporation, Sears, or Ducks Unlimited.

We all know that Christians of the first few centuries refused to serve in the army of the Roman empire, less because such work required them to spill barbarian blood than because it required them to worship a false imperial god. The urgency of such a refusal escapes us today because we are formed by a culture that regards religion as an essentially private (and consequently trivial) matter. Because our culture has so successfully domesticated Christianity, Christians tend to overestimate the importance of civility, and Thou Shalt Be Nice, though unwritten, has become the first commandment from which all the others flow.

Finding Fault

We've come to see our Church too much as those outside it see it: a thing which provides a personal commodity, a thing which underwrites the satisfaction of some private and inarticulable desire. And if that is all the Church is, then it stands to reason that the State should purchase such commodities as revelation, mercy, the Word of God, the Body and Blood of Christ, and the Truth for the soldiers of its armies. In the same way, the State provides them medical and dental care, food, clothing, AIDS testing, condoms, and movies.

Soldiers, sailors and fliers all need God's grace no less than the people they are supposed to defend. None of us, to be sure, *deserves* the Word and the Eucharist, but if Christianity can be said to bestow a "right" to anything, it is surely the right to hear that word and eat that meal. But provision of that right isn't the responsibility of the State.

Should American warriors be accompanied on the battlefield by Catholic priests? You bet your bottom Bronze Star they should. Priests are the Lord's agents, and precisely because they are the Lord's agents, they must be prepared to walk with all those whom the Lord loves. But the integrity of their ministry requires that they be unfettered by any nation's chain of command. They must *walk* with God's people, not march with them. At their ordination, at their baptism, in fact, they were mustered into an army that demands of its soldiers an absolute and undivided allegiance.

And that army so disrespects rank that its Com-

Michael O. Garvey

mander in Chief allowed raw recruits to betray and abandon him. It so disrespects national borders that its lieutenants don't bother to disguise their purpose to conquer in the name of the same Commander every human being in the world. Its soldiers are commanded not to kill others, but to die for them. They are known to rescue victims, true, but often by becoming victims themselves. Their bizarre tactic is not to subdue nations, but to break hearts.

Such is the army to which every priest (if not every Christian), whether he likes it or not, already belongs. It's not easy to understand how one man can serve in two armies without being a traitor to one of them. Unless, of course, one of the armies is merely metaphorical.

Beware of Trojans Bearing Gifts

THE issue was whether or not television networks and/or their affiliates should be permitted to sell commercial time for the advertisement of condoms. The perpetually insecure American bishops, thrice jumpy when loin-related matters become public controversy, began to issue their perfunctory condemnations of the proposed rubber ads. Anything having to do with contraception instantly renders an American bishop as brave and innovative as George Bush.

Typical of (if perhaps more carefully put than) these perfunctory "condomnations" was the page-long response of Cardinal Joseph Bernardin, archbishop of Chicago. Cardinal Bernardin objected to such advertising because, he said, "I cannot support advertising whose immediate aim is good—the prevention of disease—but which implicitly or explicitly condones promiscuity, questions the normativeness of heterosexual marriage as proper context for sexual intimacy, or artificially separates the lovemaking and life-making dimensions of marital intimacy."

Good for him, and neither could I, but so what? Leaving aside a couple of hemorrhoidal tear jerkers and the saga of that guy with the annoying laugh who bought the electric razor company there really is no other kind of advertising on prime time television.

Michael O. Garvey

Television advertisers distort and exploit sex to sell everything from Coca-Cola to Cadillacs.

And I ought to know. My wife and I clumsily preside over a turbulent household whose living room is monitored by some network outlet or other at least four hours every day; my wife has a devotion to Walter Cronkite and venerates an autograph of Charles Kuralt; my daughter is in love with Johnny Quest; my sons regularly sing the entire "This is not your father's Oldsmobile" commercial; I knew—because she looked prettier than usual—that Jane Pauley was pregnant weeks before it was announced by whoever announces such things.

When they toss the most seductive advertisements for prophylactics into the amoral and mindless vacuity that is American network television airtime, our family life won't change much. Alluring exhortations to pick up packs of Trojans will soon be part of the Musak of our imagination, along with You Deserve a Break Today and Master the Possibilities. Much worse things, I'm afraid, have already been assimilated. Much worse things soon will be. The corruption of the imagination and the imperilling of the family are among the costs you pay for living in a Burger King Town. It still beats the hell out of living, in, say, Albania.

But even so, for people who really do love sex and despise efforts to trivialize it, there was something uniquely preposterous about this particular triumph of capitalism. Something uniquely ingenious, too, about the timing of the exploiters' disingenuously logical pitch. A quite justifiable fear of AIDS had spread through the American populace without noticably affecting its promiscuity. It is a reasonable hope that the use of condoms by those many people who copulate with the carefree randomness of dogs in springtime might prevent many deaths. Most of these people are easily absorbed by television messages, and the rest of us have no right to impose our values, as the buzz phrase goes, on the poor things. America *locuta est.*

And mind you, the folks running this latest medicine show weren't in the least bit interested in making a bundle on a (pardon me) virgin advertising market. They wanted to prevent the spread of a terrifying disease was all. They wanted to educate the public. Honest.

That's why they are, even now, coming up with the brandest new brand names for their products. (I imagine it's copyrighted, but a well-known comedian has already suggested that the very name "Brooke Shields" sounds like "an anti-sexual device.") Educating consumers is, as all good adpersons know, difficult work. No more of those names based on phallic Nordic warrior fantasies; after all, these things aren't just for the scratched up vending machines in the gas station johns and the tavern pissholes any more. Now the condom market is strictly yuppie and New Age: condoms carry no-nonsense names like Mentor and Lifestyles, which appeal more to the upwardly mobile corporate back-

Michael O. Garvey

stabber, the fatuous university professor or the career-obsessed college student than to the zitfaced prom king, the booze-whacked conventioneer or the randy trucker plying some local bimbo with sloe gin fizzes. And, of course, the major networks, God bless them, will only reluctantly accept the enormous revenues generated by this new and indispensable public service.

Comparisons are always tricky, but why does all this business remind me of those pompous public statements which skin magazine editors are always making about free speech and the public's right to know? Maybe increasing numbers of sexually promiscuous citizens do, in fact, need primetime TV education about how to survive their abuse of each other by the use of rubber membrane, but it's depressing to think of how much more money and power will be obtained by the Madison Avenue sleazebags who have been encouraging the moral chaos all along.

And it's depressing to think of how the official Church, discredited by her customary clumsiness in sexual issues, will continue to make ineffectual noises as the networks and the advertising firms continue to exploit the oafish appetites of her most vulnerable children.

The Blood of Children

D URING the First World War, an enigmatic Englishman named Thomas Edward Lawrence made political history by successfully organizing several disparate Arab tribes into a revolt against the Ottoman empire and literary history by writing about it in a book titled *Seven Pillars of Wisdom*. At one point during the delicate process, while his recently formed band was resting in a place called Wadi Kitan, a quarrel erupted between a member of one clan and a member of another. There followed a fight and a killing, and after that, Lawrence, "because I was a stranger and kinless," was called upon to execute the killer.

From a tactical point of view, the execution was perfectly sensible. It would satisfy the outraged kinsmen of the victim and prevent a costly dissolution of Lawrence's growing desert army. But the strange T. E. Lawrence was a man as imaginative as he was militarily adept. He knew he was being called upon to kill an unarmed man, to participate in "the horror which would make civilized man shun justice like a plague if he had not the needy to serve him as hangmen for wages." He led the condemned man away from the camp and forced him into the back of a narrow gully.

Michael O. Garvey

Then: I stood in the entrance and gave him a few moments' delay, which he spent crying on the ground. Then I made him rise and shot him through the chest. He fell down on the weeds shrieking, with the blood coming out in spurts over his clothes, and jerked about till he rolled nearly to where I was. I fired again, but was shaking so that I only broke his wrist. He went on calling out, less loudly, now lying on his back with his feet towards me, and I leant forward and shot him for the last time in the thick of his neck under his jaw. His body shivered a little, and I called the (others), who buried him in the gully where he was. Afterwards, the wakeful night dragged over me, till, hours before dawn, I had the men up and made them load, in my longing to be set free of Wadi Kitan. They had to lift me into the saddle (*Seven Pillars of Wisdom*).

Thoughts about precisely that sort of purposeful bloodshed are difficult to avoid these days as Americans become less and less bashful about calling for the heads and hides of criminals. The secretary of defense fairly stifles a yawn as he prescribes the firing squad. A woman where I work casually favors the public castration of a recently famous rapist. Perhaps because I am a believer, I have learned to mistrust those calls to action that merely make sense. Nevertheless, they are seductive, and events in recent weeks have given all of us an abundance of them.

Finding Fault

The eyes of my four-year-old boy perceptibly widen as our chat with the man (the very kind man who gives him free pretzels all the time) behind the counter at the corner store turns to the way America's latest hostage crisis should be resolved. "I tell you what you do, Garvey," he said. "What you do is flatten Beirut one block at a time, and tough shit for the hostages. They're buzzard bait, anyhow. And tough shit for the women and kids who get in the way, too. We gotta get mean with them assholes. We gotta hit 'em where it hurts."

As he speaks, his eyes are not on mine, nor on my son's, but on the small, blue screen of the television set that keeps him company during the store's slower evening hours, and my eyes and my son's are drawn there, too. We are looking at the image of Robert Stethem, the American young man whose misfortune it has been to be associated, in the minds of a few Lebanese young men, with the U.S. Navy's shelling of Beirut. After torturing the boy, his captors have shot him in the head and thrown his corpse onto the runway tarmac.

The man behind the counter knows what I know and what all of us who have children know in a way that people without children can never know: Robert Stethem is someone's son. And the information that someone's son has been seized by strangers who have tortured and killed him is not knowledge that can be tucked away and forgotten. That blood cries out to us,

Michael O. Garvey

to the man behind the counter and to me. I suddenly need to place my hand on the warmth of my own son's cheek and to pull his head tightly against my hip.

I, a father, must admit to myself that I haven't any idea how one responds to that blood, to the blood of someone else's son. I am committing the modern, middle-class American equivalent of the sin against the Holy Spirit: handwringing. I sincerely wish I could share the decisiveness and clarity of purpose that animate those who call for quick military action based on shrewd tactical reasoning or, for that matter, the decisiveness and clarity of purpose that animate the Shiite captors armed with Korans and AK47s. They are indeed bullies and murderers, and they are sons, too.

So I stand there, mute in the corner store, hugging my son and grieving for another's son and grieving for the nameless children whose blood may soon be shed to answer his blood, and grieving for the children who have already been killed and who seem every day to be maimed and dying in the Beirut shantytowns and in the Palestinian camps and in the Israeli kibbutzim, and grieving for my own little boy who has been frightened by our bloody words and who may very well see the things that befall him in nightmares become the things that befall him in life.

I would protect him, I think, standing in a South Bend corner store, watching a dead boy's face on television and hugging my uneasy son. I would protect them all. And I know that I can't and that no one can. I ask myself how one copes with the terrible vulnerability of one's children and with the blasphemous temptation to think that this might almost be something for which God himself must be forgiven.

But I am myself a son, and from my parents I have inherited a faith, and so know that God's response to the danger has been decisive, if not obviously reassuring. He has given us yet another child, his own, to suffer and be exposed with us to a universe that includes the sober decisions of military tacticians and the screams of butchered children in the night.

On Troubled Belief

S OME local news came over the radio as I was
brushing my teeth one morning preparing to
drive my children to school before getting my wife and
myself to work. The remains of a woman killed in the
attack on Pan Am Flight 103 were being flown home to
her family in Kalamazoo, Mich. The remains of her
two-month-old baby had not yet been found. That
was all. The next story had to do with a proposed
salary increase for Congressional representatives. In
the pause, the breath, really, between the two stories, I
wondered whether the baby had been in her arms,
asleep or awake, or buckled into a safety seat next to
her; whether the explosion of the bomb had killed
them both before they began to fall. If I prayed for
them at all, it was something like a sputtered "Jesus
Christ" after spitting toothpaste and water into the
sink.

W. H. Auden wrote a poem about seeing this sort of
thing in Brueghel's depiction of the fall of Icarus,
describing how everything and everyone in the painting turns away from the tragedy, which is indicated by
a tiny, nearly unnoticeable splash. Like a brief news
item on the radio heard by a distracted man as he
brushes his teeth. The big news this morning was that I
failed to notice how a car door had been left slightly
ajar and so dented the frame of our automatic garage

94

Finding Fault

door. The curse I bellowed scared the children as well as myself, and to smooth things over, we drove to school listening to their favorite rock station play the old Kinks' hit "You Really Got Me Going." By the time we reached their school we were all singing—or shouting—the chorus at the top of our lungs, and the garage door and the curse were forgotten. As were the shattered madonna and child plummeting through the black skies over Scotland. Life is like that.

But the forgetting isn't always so easy. A headline in the same morning's *New York Times* brought the deaths to mind again: "Holding on to One's Faith in a World of Violence." It appeared above an interview with Hugh Nissenson about his new book, *The Elephant and My Jewish Problem.* Nissenson spoke about a meeting with a French Jesuit priest during the trial of Klaus Barbie. The priest told him that he believed the human condition was unchanged since Adam and Eve. The world awaited its Redeemer, and not even the murder of children shook his faith. "It cost me mine," replied Nissenson, who had covered the Eichmann trial in Jerusalem as well. There was no rebuke offered here, no judgment of the priest's integrity. Nissenson spoke of the Frenchman's "beautiful face" as indicating a profound inner spiritual struggle. "All I can say," he concluded, "is that I cannot assent." It had taken him a long time, he said, to admit to himself that he couldn't believe, "because I loved the belief."

In the wake of the Pan Am bombing, there are surely

Michael O. Garvey

believers who don't love their belief, those who both
believe in God *and* cannot assent. Those who shudder
at the proximity between the Nativity and the Massa-
cre of the Innocents and the inevitable association of
the two events. Those trying to be attentive to the
Cross who find themselves simply stupefied surrounding it. Believers who wonder: Two months old. Had
she been breast- or bottle-feeding the baby? Were the
grandparents waiting at the airport in Kalamazoo
when word came of the disaster? Where was the
baby's father? Where was God? For those believers it's
not easy to say which is the more dreadful thing, the
inflection or the innuendo. The mother and baby
dashed to pieces in Scotland or the breezy announce-
ment of it on the morning news. The horror inflicted in
the night sky or the muttered reaction of a man spitting into a sink. The disaster or the nonchalant turning
away from it. Paul once wrote to some people in Phi-
lippi, doing his level best to be encouraging, but finally telling them that they must work out their own
salvation in fear and trembling, knowing that it was
God who worked in them, inspiring both the will and
the deed for God's own chosen purpose.

Perhaps God inspires the will to hunt down, root
out and destroy the thing, whatever it is—whether in
the world or in a human soul—in the name of which a
child could be murdered and the murder of children
could be forgotten. But a violent world offers neither
the equipment nor the cunning for such a chase.

So believers with little love for the belief, surrepti-

Finding Fault

tious believers who cannot assent, are left with violence and silence. The fiery deaths, the dazed families,
the mangled hearts of those who willed and built and
planted the bomb, their own despair all seem to them a
sort of imaginative and vulnerable void into which the
impulse of faith must be smuggled, pregnant with its
own sort of explosion.

Making the Hard Choices

REAL-TIME ultrasound technology has been used with increasing frequency since its invention in 1976. From a transmitter placed on the surface of the abdomen, sound waves flood the womb, make contact with its occupant and provide a computer with the information necessary to project on a television screen a surprisingly detailed image. Ultrasound is only one of the most conspicuous and impressive advances in a new and burgeoning science called fetology, which enables a mother's physician to treat her developing child as a "second patient."

As more is learned about the unborn's life and environment, more can be done to bring him or her to a healthy and hopeful birth. As the womb has become less mysterious to the life scientist, lifesaving therapy and even surgery for the children who live there have become possible and might soon become routine. As more attention is paid to children before their birth, their membership in the community outside the womb and the respect that membership obligates should become more apparent.

For all who have understood that children, born and preborn, are by far the most unjustly treated, most continually exploited and most routinely butchered class of human beings on this planet, the expansion of fetology is welcome indeed.

Finding Fault

My own first encounter with fetology was late one Halloween night, after an 80-mile ambulance ride. It seemed possible that two people, and quite likely that one person, would die that night. Moments before an emergency cesarean section, a very wise doctor sought to slow the alarming ascent of my wife's blood pressure by placing in her hands a microphone that emitted the frantic, but sturdy, heartbeat of a 3-pound, 7-ounce little boy. He survived and is now responsible for most of Indiana's dairy industry. His parents will never forget the first time they heard his heart beat.

On two other, less alarming occasions, we took advantage of the science by watching, on real-time ultrasound, the images of our two other children and having things explained to us by an obviously amused obstetrician who was, the previous time, unable to obtain for us the bet-settler that a delighted and relieved but impolite Mrs. Garvey called a "crotch-shot."

Recently, with the aid of real-time ultrasound, we saw a child we didn't know seized, quartered, decapitated and sucked down a vacuum tube in a film titled "Silent Scream." The child's head (for which the technicians of abortion employ the euphemism "number one"—as when an anesthesiologist asks the surgeon, "Is number one out yet?" had to be crushed to permit its evacuation. Even before the killing, as the tip of the suction tube probed the cervix and found its defenseless target, the child stiffened in what seemed remarkably like fright at the approach of something alien. We learned that the child's heartbeat had increased to

Michael O. Garvey

nearly 200 beats a minute, and I remembered again the first time I heard my little boy's heart. In a frantic attempt to escape the suction tube, this child began to pound against the uterine walls with what looked like a born child's terror. The child's mouth opened seconds before the end in what looked like an already born person's scream.

We were watching a dilation and curettage abortion performed 12 weeks into an unwanted pregnancy, the most common sort. When uninvited children deleriously seek membership in American society, this is the way they are ordinarily dealt with. A very lucrative industry has grown up around the process, and about three such abortions occur every minute in the hundreds of centers that now dot the American landscape. One such place was recently established within a few hundred feet of the backyard where our own children play. Abortion has become as American a practice as eating Chicken McNuggets. Nobody forces anybody into McDonald's restaurants and nobody forces anybody into abortion clinics, the conventional argument goes, so the opponent of either should mind his or her own business. Period. In the mid-19th century, Americans were encouraged to think similarly about the practice of buying and selling black people. From time to time, Americans are encouraged to think this way about various institutions such as prostitution, the drug market and child pornography. It's a healthy democratic instinct to recoil from any proposal of coercion, and proponents of abortion on demand

Finding Fault

have been quick to capitalize on that instinct. Do *you* think you have the right to force a woman to bear the child you don't know and she doesn't want?

It's a terribly, terribly complex issue, I'm told. I'm a man, I'm told, and so will never know what bearing and rearing a child is like. I will never need to make that terrible choice, I'm told. And I'm told that if abortion is made illegal again, desperate women will again be driven to seek the sleazy services of clumsy underworld abortionists. I'm told that the poorest women will be made poorer unless they are able to obtain efficient and sanitary abortions, that my own daughter may someday be pregnant as a result of rape, that making abortions illegal is yet another attempt to subjugate women, that abortion is sometimes the most compassionate decision, that it is as complex an issue as it is tragic. I'm told all these things, and I try to keep them in mind.

I don't know the woman who obtained the abortion in the film, and I don't know why she did. I don't know the man who impregnated her, and I don't know whether he shared in the decision. I don't know the home in which the child might have lived, and I don't know whether the child might gradually have become welcome there. What I do know is this, that a child secure in its mother's womb was discovered, attacked, pursued and ripped apart; that the child seemed aware of its doom and died in terror; and that the one clear reason for this was that the child was not desired.

Abortion is a complex issue. Everyone knows that.

Michael O. Garvey

Everyone but its first victims. In the film, I caught a glimpse of the issue from their point of view, which is, after all, less sophisticated than ours and less alert to complexity.

Nobody had consulted the condemned child on the terribly intricate, terribly anguished and paradoxically compassionate moral decision that resulted in its killing. But then again, children (like all weak people) don't have the equipment to make the really hard choices. Strong people, people like us, usually know what's best for them, and we act accordingly.

Until Children Are Safe

D ANIEL C. MAGUIRE, a theologian frequently
quoted by "pro-choice" advocates in the abortion war, once wrote and published a remarkable
account of a visit he paid to an abortion-providing
agency called the Milwaukee Women's Health Organization. For me, the most memorable moments in the
article had to do with Maguire's handling and evaluat-
ing what I couldn't help but think of as the corpse of a
destroyed child. For me, the essay exemplified the in-
tellectual incoherence and maimed imagination which
I still believe indispensable to a tolerance of the prac-
tices condoned by the Supreme Court's recently chal-
lenged Roe v. Wade decision.

There was, in the essay, much use of euphemism:
Readers were invited to behold "aborted matter," "un-
identifiable fleshy matter," a "conceptuum," an "embryo." In its conspicuous avoidance of a precise name
for the thing an abortion destroys, the account reminded me uncomfortably of the Pentagon's Vietnam-
era "vertically deployed antipersonnel devices" and
"pacification programs."

"I have held babies in my hands," Maguire wrote.
"And now I held this embryo. I know the difference.
This had not been a person or a candidate for baptism." I certainly couldn't imagine hiring a babysitter
(nor calling on a baptist) who could write such words,

Michael O. Garvey

but it was difficult, as well, to put one's trust in a professional theologian, an ethicist for crying out loud, capable of such a chilling and absolute statement. I had assumed that ethicists were more open-minded than that.

While not presuming to speak for the Church, as Maguire has said those Catholics who disagree with him do, I would at least argue that his certainty is not available to many of us who oppose current abortion law and practice. We revere "selves," not "stages," and while we lament the chaos and anguish that result from an undesired pregnancy or from the birth of a blighted child, we simply cannot bring ourselves to agree that unwanted strangers are best dealt with by killing.

Maguire wrote movingly, if confusingly, of a woman who elected to abort because her "life situation was seriously incompatible with parenting" (a fact made sadly obvious by her decision, when you thought about it) and because she "could not bear the thought of adoption." But that was not surprising. Few parents can bear the thought of their own children in irretrievable exile, and parents have been known to become deranged when threatened by such suffering. Their understandable and utterly justifiable fear gives rise to a spurious decisiveness. But tequila, consumed in sufficient quantities, can give rise to spurious decisiveness in the operator of an automobile, too. Neither the fear nor the drunkenness justifies a lethal result.

Finding Fault

As a lay Catholic, I don't claim to speak for the Church, but I can speak for a large Catholic community that has a long tradition of welcoming strangers and giving them a home, and of holding itself up to judgment for the quality of that welcome; a community that has always believed that Jesus approaches us most often as a stranger; a community which has learned painfully that the extent to which we close our homes and hearts and lives to others and, yes, especially to children, is precisely the extent to which we have placed ourselves beyond the reach of a loving God; a community which knows the truth of Dostoyevski's observation that love in practice is a harsh and dreadful thing, and that knows that to love is often—no, always—to bear the cross.

Maguire, in his book *A New American Justice* (Winston Press, 1980) once wrote, "Justice untouched by mercy is minimalistic and stinting in its response to persons. Justice is incipient love and thus has some native ties to generosity and enthusiasm. A society whose 'justice' is calculating, cold and miserly will not rise to the needs of persons." I think that is very well said. It is precisely the reason I believe that a society that must first recognize "a candidate for baptism" (or any other such stage) before extending a minimal justice to a developing child by suffering that child to be born, is a society which has declared all the weak—the terrified, potential mothers; the mad; the feebleminded; the wretched; the lonely; the friendless,

Michael O. Garvey

broken and confused—as its enemies. In such a society, those most in need of mercy will find none.

I suppose many of us have seemed quarrelsome and unfair to Maguire and other "pro-choice" advocates; and indeed we may, on occasion, have been too quick to denounce and reprehensibly reluctant to listen to the counterarguments. But our concerns, at least until very recently, have been too often shouted down and misrepresented.

Think about it: We see ourselves surrounded by a culture that despises our children and other vulnerable people. Unless we march in lockstep with the National Organization of Women, we are accused of marching lockstep with a reactionary and sexist administration in Rome. Unless we swallow, like some bad clam, the destruction of one and a half million children a year, we are accused of hostility to the one and a half million women who yearly patronize the abortion industry. Unless we are mute, ignoring the carnage that enriches that industry, we are called exploitative. We try to be civil, but all of this becomes annoying.

Proponents of present day abortion policy should keep these things in mind. They should also know that, while we bear them no ill will, our society will not be tranquil as long as that diabolical industry is allowed to flourish. We won't yield, we won't be silent, we won't go away, we won't rest until we believe children are safe.

Where Children Are Safe

I T HAS always been dangerous to be a little person in a society of big people. Herod's memorandum to the Roman garrison at Bethlehem gave us only one memorable example of what can happen when children too obviously impede the career interests of adults. The widespread, contemporary and legally protected practice of killing off inconvenient unborn and blighted children is another.

Unfortunately, the most conspicuous witness on behalf of little people is too often given by, well, *distracted* bigger ones, folks who seem to see in today's horrendous slaughter little more than the opportunity to make a point about (pick at least one) the rosary, the pope, natural family planning, Geraldine Ferraro, Our Lady of Fatima, the People's Republic of China, sex, Andrew Greeley, the University of Notre Dame, women, Phil Donahue, sexism, the Bible, the sexual revolution, lesbianism, AIDS, George Bush and the cardinal archbishop of Boston.

Except as an emotive noise, the word "child" seems unimportant in their arguments. A boorish "pro-life" advocate in Chicago, for instance, recently gained much publicity by using a megaphone from a nearby house to harass a pregnant and terrified child whose parents were contemplating, or so he seemed to have reason to believe, procurement of an abortion. His

Michael O. Garvey

alleged concern was the welfare of a baby (which baby was unclear), but publicity was apparently what he was after, and what he gained.

But there is another kind of witness—one more costly, less cowardly and more immediately recognizable as Christian. That is the witness of Our Lady of the Wayside, a Catholic Worker House in Avon, Ohio, where a few of those children who have managed to escape the contemporary final solution are alive, beloved and loving.

The mistress of this hopeful, odd and unpredictable household is Dorothy Gauchat, a "first generation" Catholic Worker, a beautiful and plainspoken daughter of the Midwest, a treasure of the church and, as you might have guessed, a person about whom it is impossible for me to write without wearing my heart on my sleeve. Her husband, Bill, who died in 1975, founded the Blessed Martin de Porres Cleveland Catholic Worker House in 1939. It was there that Dorothy, then a high-school girl, met and fell in love with him. Much of the story of their remarkable marriage and family, and of the way their Catholic Worker household evolved from the conventional sort into its present form, is told in Dorothy Gauchat's splendid little book, *All God's Children* (Ballantine, $2.50).

Our Lady of the Wayside is home for about 90 people, most of them children who need special care. Some of the children are outcasts. Others have loving families that, for a variety of reasons, are unable to take care of their children alone. Children with spina bifida, children who are hydrocephalic, children with Down's syndrome, children with brain damage, children damaged by their mothers' drug abuse. About the only thing the children at Dorothy Gauchat's house have in common is that she loves them and acts upon her love.

The very phrase "meaningful human life" has always baffled Dorothy Gauchat. She regularly celebrates the Eucharist with children whose lives are not, by the standards of contemporary fashion, meaningful. She and they assist one another in giving glory to God, support one another in faith, endure together in hope, love one another. It is a judgment on a godforsaken, yuppie-ridden society that none of these activities makes a compelling claim—at least none that law or custom will defend vigorously—to be meaningfully human. The people who live at Our Lady of the Wayside are outcasts in this profoundest sense.

According to our faith, human life is inviolable not so much because it is inherently sacred as because God alone is its maker and master. Our reverence for one another is meant less to express the truth about us than to express the truth about God.

Grace in Manhattan

"CHILDREN must take a lot of time," she said. To a city-stunned son of the Midwest with toddler barf drying on the lapels of his hand-me-down tweed jacket, she seemed intimidatingly Manhattanite, this attractive and hyperarticulate video producer. She was the shackup, girlfriend, spouse-equivalent, or whatever New Yorkers call them these days, of a high-school classmate, and we were eating complicated Italian dishes with other classmates and good friends in a lower East side restaurant. She was being kind, charitably searching for some way to secure my participation in a conversation which had suddenly gone so glittery and arcane as to be incomprehensible.

She was politely commenting on a worn color snapshot which had been passed around the table when another classmate had asked for descriptions of the kids. Not really knowing what to say about the time children took, what they took the time from, and what astonishing things they reveal about time, I said, "Yeah, I guess they do." Helping myself to the antipasto, I thought guiltily of my wife, who would have been, at that moment, pinned down in our sonorous, high-ceilinged upstairs bathroom, singlehandedly maneuvering three shrieking timebandits through their pre-Walt Disney movie ritual sheepdip. "They take a lot," I added.

Finding Fault

Yesterday, the day I'd left for New York, our first-grader had been frightened by a bully on the playground. Losing track of the tabletalk, I began to remember how his eyes had looked when he'd told me about the incident, how full of worry and wonder and bravery. He'd take our advice and tell the teacher next time, he'd told us. But in those amazing eyes I could see dread that a time would come . . . perhaps not now, but inevitably, when he would in some sense have to stand his ground; a dawning realization that we, his parents, could offer him only feeble protection from an unreliable and sometimes predatory world, a world where people could be cruel for the sheer hell of it, where bullies were often left free to terrorize the vulnerable. In his little boy's eyes, I thought I'd caught a glimpse of the strange and admirable man he would become. To think about the things children took! The video producer was asking an abstract question or two about what children involved, as if about a stock option or the fauna on Saturn, and I resisted a sudden urge to excuse myself for a quick phone call home.

The New Yorkers all began to talk about how little time they had, and I began to feel as if I were trapped in a Woody Allen screenplay. I *knew* these guys, and I knew very well that they had a few months apiece more discretionary time than even the most selfpitying university professor in South Bend, Indiana. I knew no person at the table who was ever obliged to work outside the hours roughly bookended by eight o'clock in the morning and five o'clock in the evening. I knew

111

Michael O. Garvey

no person at the table who had a spouse. I knew no person at the table who could not reasonably claim any evening hours as his or her own. None of these people was a doctor, none had developed a reputation for heroic round-the-clock service to people in need, and none was at work on a symphony or a novel. None of these people lived with a child. So where was this time hemorrhage? And would somebody please pass me the bardolino? Somebody did, and I poured a little, and we drank to our friendship, which had deep roots in a special region of our own childhood.

All of us had spent our adolescence together in a claustral New England boarding school contending with the intense guardianship of a few English Benedictine monks whose communal rule required them— and, by extension, us—to revere time. Despite the exotic mixture of monasticism and preppiness in which we'd been embedded, we enjoyed, I suppose, a pretty conventional North American late childhood for the times. Like teenagers who lived at home, we exaggerated the harshness of the regimen imposed on us. We surreptitiously disqualified ourselves for future Supreme Court appointments. We surrendered our imaginations to the collective enchantment of that white, middle-class, suburban phenomenon which was briefly thought of as a counterculture. And several of us, including those reunited here in this Manhattan restaurant, came to love each other. Which is why we were, not painfully, but awkwardly, forced to pay respectful attention to each other.

Finding Fault

I guess I envied them a little. The enormity of their freedom, the pure possibility which charged every moment of their frenzied urban life, the disposable incomes which allowed them frequent access to such splendid Italian food as this and good times as these. Earlier that evening, various telephone answering machines around Manhattan having reached a consensus on time and place, we had all hopped into taxis and arrived here. At home, such a gathering would have required more planning than an international summit conference. The schedules of a husband, a wife, a babysitter, three children, two schools, and one church would need to be harmonized before time and place could be reasonably discussed.

And I guess they envied me, too. The claims of family meant that my anguish (aside from the usual fear of the Four Last Things) could be sharply focused and quickly inventoried: The vulnerability of my wife and children, the integrity of my marriage, and bills. That was pretty much it. Not so for them. And they had anguish by the soul-load. In fact, I suspect that they complained so anomalously about dwindling time precisely because of the intensity of their anguish, the way shocked survivors of some plane crash might mutter loonily about a connecting flight they fear to miss.

Because they were thinking, as I often do—as, I suppose, most people of our mid-thirtyish age naturally begin to do—about death. About the fact that there will too soon come a time, with or without the nuclear

Michael O. Garvey

conflagration, the AIDS epidemic, the ruptured ozone
layer, the diagnosis of cancer, the fatal mugging, the
cocaine overdose, or the car accident, when we will
not be alive any more. Blood will stop dancing along
our arterial corridors; wind will no longer rush in and
out of our lungs; our senses will blink out one by one;
our knowledge of self and other and perhaps even our
deepest yearning will inevitably recede. Those dearest
to us may be at hand to pity us as we suffer and die and
to speak fondly of us afterwards, but soon they, too
will die, and we and they will be forgotten, and, eventually, the whole planet and the star at the center of
our planetary family and the galaxy in which that star
is one insignificant mote in a few trillion, all of that,
and whatever may be left of us along with all of that,
will fade. It's just not right that we have so little control over what happens between now and then. It's unfair, as Wallace Stevens wrote, "that we live in a place
that is not our own, and much more, not ourselves/
and hard it is in spite of blazoned days." It's unfair that
we have so goddam little time.

I think we were all thinking about that as our conversation faltered and as we found ourselves smiling
shyly among each other in the warm candlelight. As
teenagers together, we had affected a kind of hip alienation in the hope that it might emphasize our particu-
larity, outrage our monastic elders, and impress those
sophisticated girls on whom we had crushes. But now
our affectations were returning to haunt us. It no
longer seemed important to outrage the monks, nor to

114

Finding Fault

impress sophisticated girls, nor to draw attention to oneself. But with all of these things faded, the alienation was still there. We were men approaching middle age and feeling mortal. We still lived in a place that was not our own and not ourselves. We would die and be forgotten there.

I think some of us were thinking about how nonchalant and frail were the agreements which kept us and our lovers together, and how paradoxically constrictive, too. Most of us had daily to renegotiate these agreements in which there could never be room for a child. Some of us knew that the disturbance of children was a sacred message which whole lives had to be arranged to receive; that the cry of a baby was the voice of God, assuring us that this "place that is not our own" belongs to him.

One friend and fellow veteran of a billion sophomoric bull sessions on the meaning of life, death, sex and human striving goaded me congenially. Tell us about marriage and kids and bowling and Indiana, he said. I retorted with some jeer about insightful yuppies, and we all laughed. I suppose he really might have wanted me to say something earnest about the virtues of ordinary Midwestern married life and about the rapacious folly of New York. But I couldn't have managed it.

In that pleasant restaurant, drinking good red wine, we all avoided speaking too directly about these things, but we seemed to be telling each other that even in this hallucinatory plight of mortality and

Michael O. Garvey

garlic bread, in these blazoned days, we loved and pitied each other. It was good to be together there no matter what else was said, and while I fretted about my wife and my kids and my friends and their companions it was also good to know that grace, if not children, could flourish in affluent Manhattan.

Downstairs in the Household of Faith

C AN nothing be done to spare us these remind-ers? At a press conference one summer in Rome, a Vatican spokesman insisted that 16th-century Catholic teaching on indulgences, notwithstanding its sometimes bizarre implications of how God wields his mercy, is "unrenounceable and immutable." He was talking about 16th-century teaching on *indulgences*, remember; not 16th-century teaching on the real presence of the body and blood and soul and divinity of our Lord in the Eucharist, but about how you can add three years' supply of flame retardant to the tank on your purgatorial fire extinguisher by reciting the Memorare.

This pressing issue was raised during an unabashed discussion of the conditions under which Catholics could be granted plenary indulgences through the medium of television by prayerfully watching pontifical Masses and blessings. A *New York Times* writer gleefully quoted the Rev. Luigi De Magistris of the Sacred Apostolic Penitentiary as saying: "It's got to be a live transmission. Watching a replay is not sufficient."

Did the Monsignor *have* to say it just that confidently? There, in the July 18 edition of *The New York Times*, for all the world to read? There, in *The Times*, whose editors already seem so eager to portray our Church as a murky empire of bead-telling, miracle-

117

Michael O. Garvey

mongering, Latin-muttering, bingo-card-shuffling, garlic-chewing, woman-hating, sex-obsessed, Vatican-owned-and-operated papal groupies; who insist on calling us not Catholics, as we call ourselves, but *Roman* Catholics; who fault our bishops' letter on war and peace for pretending the nation could "hide in" morality when the point was being made that the nation couldn't hide *from* it; and who consistently report on our efforts (and any others, for that matter) in behalf of the unborn as if these were based not on gratitude for the mysterious and invaluable gift of the human being, but on a combination of institutional misogyny and disgust at orgasm.

The frequency with which the Church rushes to accommodate these silliest stereotypes is embarrassing, of course, but it is also darkly consoling to remember that the rotten eggs that splatter on our institutional walls are most often thrown by relatively unimaginative folks whose hopes and desires have gone boring and flabby on them, their ghastliest nightmares featuring terminal gum disease and an unflat tummy.

But what do such people actually know of our Catholic predicament? What do they know about being God's own bewildered gate-crashers in a two-millenia-long universal hide-and-seek party organized by the Blessed Trinity? What do they know about the anguish of living in the last days and trying to knit together a loving family with Mary, the Mother of God, my Uncle Mike, Phil Donahue, Phyllis Schlafly, Bernard of Clairvaux, Mary Daly, Luigi De Magistris,

Finding Fault

Dan Berrigan, Charlemagne, Walker Percy, Joseph Ratzinger, Soeur Sourire, Andrew Greeley, Teresa of Calcutta, Francis of Assisi, Pio Nono and the double-tonsured cosmonaut in the Hawaiian shirt who sits in the pew in front of mine at Mass and flashes a "Sieg Heil" salute during the Our Father?

But let's face it: the barnacled curial bureaucracy in Rome and the noisy diaspora of high-strung conservative cultists—who seem to believe that the Holy Spirit is mute and powerless in the absence of curial clearance—have not exactly monopolized the power to make a Catholic layman wince. Every kook in Christendom seems to be getting in on the action. My nephew, a splendid and impeccably honest young man, recently swore to me that he had survived a day-long retreat during which he and a dozen of his Catholic high school classmates were subjected to a fascinating catechesis on the sacrament of reconciliation. The retreat directors separated the (involuntary and sullen . . . some things never change) adolescent retreatants into groups of 10 and had them walk laps of the school gymnasium with one representative of each group carrying a pebble in his shoe. Exactly why in the hell, I asked my nephew, did they do that? It baffled him, too, he admitted, although he added with characteristic good nature and tolerance that the consequent lap-limping probably had something to do with bearing crosses or troubles or perhaps even sins through one's life. Or something. After this exercise, my nephew and the others were taken into the school chapel and ex-

119

posed to a form of communal penance in which they wrote down terse descriptions of their sins on scraps of paper and proceeded to a brazier on the altar where the scraps were burned as the theme song for the movie *Chariots of Fire* was played on a compact disk. Perhaps this is the Southern Californian mutation of the problem of Msgr. Luigi De Magistris and the Apostolic Penitentiary.

These preposterous displays of ecclesial hijinks, Roman and home-grown, are pretty much what the world sees of us these days. Disconcerted as most of us are by this entire crazorama, we might be able to find something encouraging in our embarrassment. Perhaps we find all this public chatter about indulgences humiliating because it comes from within our own household. It exposes a quaint familial peculiarity that most of us are willing to . . . well, to indulge, even if it requires us to pretend for the benefit of a few weirdos that God is as anal retentive as they are, but which we would just as soon not discuss in front of the already jeering pagans. Perhaps our anguish over the spat between Cardinal Ratzinger and Father Curran is that neither man seems able to speak for a family of faith whose wisdom we know to be far richer, more life-giving, and just plain more interesting that all that smoke they are blowing about the location of authority and the limits of dissent. Perhaps we become depressed when we see the most juvenile examples of pop psychology presented in place of the sacrament of reconciliation, because in that sacrament we ourselves have

Finding Fault

learned the true terrors of sin and now know what it is like to be pursued to the roots of one's being and forgiven.

Probably because it is made up of us, the Church reminds us of too much. We (we individuals; we, the Church; and we and the Church) *say* that we are awaiting Christ's return, but here we all are reading advertisements for videocassette recorders, or issuing statements on contraception, or having affairs, or calculating indulgences, or carping about tenure, or avoiding panhandlers, or lobbing dogmas around like hand grenades, or denying our time to spouses and kids, or watching the David Letterman Show, or, really, doing anything at all to distract ourselves from the inconvenient and incarnate and obstinate Word.

Membership in a Church that is so radically nonchalant about what the dying world holds dearest (borders, armies, states, money, tribes, power, security and stuff like that) has never been entirely comfortable. We should not become too exasperated that the Church's rather flexible house rules have always given an edge to the loonies among us because they (both the loonies and the rules) at the very least guarantee that we will approach and engage contemporary culture on terms other than its own. When you think about that culture's ability to produce Cabbage Patch Kids, Madonna, MasterCard, Planned Parenthood and the Trident submarine, you glimpse the value of that guarantee.

For us sinners in search of the Risen Jesus, this is

Michael O. Garvey

the muddle, this is the quirky history, these are the brothers and sisters, this is the household we are stuck with. In moments of alarm and stress, we may forget our gripes and huddle together; in moments of great joy we may want everybody to link arms; and in the warmth of too much drink we may grudgingly declare our undying love for one another. But this side of the Lord's return will always be a mess.

Instead of losing sleep over our institutional preoccupations with authority and sex, the irrelevance of our hierarchy's loyal opposition, and the recent fluffiness of our kids' formal indoctrination, we might fret some more about our own quickness to judge, hardness of heart and lack of focus.

How can we be saved when we cannot even seem to pay enough attention to notice our peril? Between our customary ways of making do and what we know has happened in Christ's Incarnation there yawns a massive and scary abyss. We are no dopes, so rather than wringing our hands and begging for insight, we keep busy on its edge. We prefer our own need to be right to the truth, ignore those in most immediate need of us, multiply our appetites, obtain more leverage, accumulate more power and bitch about who's in charge of doctrine, all the while demanding that the Church ("it," or "they," in this case, not "we") somehow ratify, excuse or endorse the folly that keeps us on this side. We know and the example of Club Med suggests that any institutional arrangement accommodating escapism is necessarily weird, so it should not surprise

Finding Fault

us, sinners that we are, when our church's most officious custodians and flamboyant critics (every mother's child among us has at some time been one or the other) sometimes come across as the feeblest of all.

Whether or not we enjoy living like cosmic gypsies, we have, as the manual says, no abiding city here, and that should suit us fine. After all, others claimed the whole enterprise was looking pretty hopeless long before the pontificate of Pope Pius XII, when I was drafted into it. As the Son of God walked with them toward torture and execution in Jerusalem, his closest friends amused themselves by arguing about their own local distractions and foolishness. It took a Resurrection to break into their hearts for a moment or two. It still does. It always will.

Here Lies a Priest of Jesus Christ

I T WAS one of those startling sights which the parents of startling young children come to find commonplace: an eight-year-old boy in bed, still sound asleep in the morning sunlight, curled up with a replica of an Andalusian bull. Wrapped around this replica, was a piece of notebook paper on which, during the night, he had emblazoned a purple cross and inscribed, "I miss you."

My son had been given this odd version of a teddy-bear by his great uncle, Michael Owen Driscoll, a priest, and a man who loved bullfights. Michael Francis loves bullfights, too, and loves the man who gave him this somewhat grotesque and anatomically correct souvenir of one. He was grieving for his great uncle. He missed Tio, as our family called him.

I miss Tio, too. How can I not miss the guy who used to entertain us, his horrified nephews and nieces, with such spinetingling and absurd stories as "Ding-Dong Donald;" who taught me how to swim; who once let a bored ten-year-old nephew stay up all night in his chancery office apartment watching "The Untouchables" and trying out cigarettes; who regularly delighted and scared my own kids by sending them a postcard of Goya's "Saturn Devouring his Children," whose body was waked in the church he built, with his chalice at the coffin's head and a crate of Mars Bars for

124

Finding Fault

the parish children at its foot? Tio was enough of a
child himself to enjoy a special rapport with children. I
remember watching him train altar servers once, im-
perious in his red-buttoned cassock, and shouting im-
patiently at one of them, "Turn to the right, Bobby!
To the right! Look, Bobby: Hold up the finger that
you pick your nose with. That's your right hand. Got
it?"

Monsignor Michael Owen Driscoll, pastor of Our
Savior's Parish in Jacksonville, Ill., died late on
Pentecost Sunday or early the next morning. On Pentecost, he had presided at a First Communion Mass
and he was within weeks of his retirement. We grieving relatives have been reminding each other that retirement is something for which Tio seemed particularly unsuited.

According to family lore, my great grandfather, Michael Owen Driscoll, Tio's grandfather, was wounded
defending the integrity of the Union at the battle of
Gaines Mill, near Antietam, by a Confederate bullet
which struck him square in the heel. I remember many
hilarious dinners at which Tio speculated that since
our ancestor's wound indicated the likelihood that his
back had been turned on a rebel enfilade, "heel" might
have been a euphemism to mitigate the shame of what
was possibly a headlong retreat. He laughed loudly
(his was a wonderful, contagious, thunderclapping
sort of laughter) and mocked his grandfather affectionately, in much the same way he ribbed his contemporary relations, and one imagines that Great

Michael O. Garvey

Grandpa Driscoll wouldn't mind it any more than I, his namesake, did. In any event, it's difficult to imagine Tio retreating from anything or anyone.

The present cultural climate admonishes us to be cautious about recently conventional notions of masculinity. Nevertheless, I will always remember this larger than life, chain-smoking, wine-quaffing, table pounding, ultramontane, utterly argumentative character with the great bulging eyes and the booming voice, this guy who seemed to regard every encounter as, first and foremost, a potential outrage, as among the manliest of men.

In the days shortly before the outbreak of the Second World War, not long before he was ordained and while he was still in the Roman seminary, Tio went on an excursion to Paris, where he and his brother, John, pubcrawled through a particularly—well, secular— section of the city. In a bar there, wearying of the loud, widely addressed and virulently anti-Semitic remarks of another tourist, a German army officer at a nearby table, Tio contributed a haymaker which sent the Nazi through a plateglass window, squared the consequent bill with the delighted proprietor, and strolled out of the place minutes before the gendarmes arrived. Direct, abrupt and unambivalent action was Tio's style, whether at work or at play, a predilection so pronounced as to blur the distinction between work and play, in fact. One of his many passions (along with Church history, opera, St. Louis Cardinals base-

Finding Fault

ball, Shakespeare, Dante, good red wines and late Renaissance painting) was bullfighting, probably because of its delicate blend of recreation and seriousness. He ridiculed Ernest Hemingway's writing and self-apotheosis, but Tio's figure and Hemingway's do invite comparison.

Don't get me wrong. We're not talking about Rambo here, but we're not talking about some reprehensibly sensitive product of zeitgeist, either. One of Tio's favorite descriptions of Jesus is a line from Ezra Pound: "No capon priest was our Goodly Fere, but a man among men was He." Tio was no capon priest. Nor was he a "mouse of the scrolls" as he frequently accused me of being, particularly when we disagreed on anything having to do with the Church, which was nearly every time we spoke. "Namesake," he would thunder in response to some mildly advanced opinion about the implementation of Vatican II, "that is nothing but a bunch of theology!" His tone would convey little reverence for the queen of the sciences. Most contemporary theologians, according to Tio's ecclesiology, were effete, sidelined, meddling wackos. He and his brother parish priests (a group which could, individually and collectively, always count on his unconditional loyalty) were busy in the vineyard while those eggheads were yammering about collegiality and such. I looked forward to and could count on an abusive phone call from Tio whenever a piece with my name at the bottom appeared in the NCR. ("I'll tell you

Michael O. Garvey

where all you liberal guys really miss the boat, Namesake . . .") He welcomed many of the conciliar changes much as a hassled, veteran street cop would accept Miranda regulations. His notion of lay ministry was that which ushers and altar and rosary society volunteers did. His response to the idea of ordaining women to the priesthood: "I've got two words for that: Forget it." His response to the idea of ordaining married people is unprintable here.

The people in his parish loved him as much as he loved them, which is to say unreservedly. We in Tio's family saw this through our own tears as we wept with them during Tio's funeral. *Ubi caritas et amor, Deus ibi est.* The mutual love of this community and its often autocratic and occasionally grumpy pastor is the place where God is. It is what the Church is for. Tio was right, I suppose: All the rest is a bunch of theology. Which might be why he elected to be buried under a stone on which is inscribed not his name, but simply "Here lies the body of a priest of Jesus Christ."

His favorite painting hung across the room from the easychair to which his failing health increasingly confined Monsignor Michael Owen Driscoll for the last few years. It is El Greco's Saint Peter at prayer, weeping, bewildered, and clutching the keys to the kingdom. Doubtless, the papacy will never again have an adherent as uncritical as Tio, but I know (because we talked about it often) that what fascinated Mike Driscoll most of all about El Greco's painting was not its symbolism. It was Peter's eyes, and the recognition

Finding Fault

of an overwhelming mercy which burned in them. Whether at play with his nephews and nieces or at work as a parish priest, Tio's whole life was a celebration of confidence in that mercy.

What a blessing to have such a man for an uncle!

Zipadeedoodah

SAP'S RISING. Birds are chirping. The red robin is bob bob bobbin' along, and just this morning you saw in your back yard what will soon be a host of golden daffodils.

It's spring, boys and girls, and the world is mud luscious and puddle wonderful, and each mortal thing is dealing out that being indoors each one dwells, and e.e. cummings is in heaven with Gerard Manley Hopkins, and there is an ample hunk of Easter season left, and you're thinking about Resurrection. You are walking not to Emmaus but to work, which is really the same thing, head down, admiring the pool of sky in each specular mudpuddle alongside the road, whistling Zipadeedoodah, kicking up spray after idle spray of cinders and waiting for a sign from God. Haven't you, after all, every right to expect one? There is nothing like the convergence of Easter, a fine spring morning, a loving household, a sweet leavetaking and a tasty breakfast to exacerbate your natural inclination to outrageous presumption.

You recollect yourself momentarily with an inward wince, like a man remembering a drunken moment, a blurting out of something silly to a woman he has long admired from afar. Something like: "I can't stand it any longer, this not begging you to marry me, I mean. Come with me now. We'll drive all day and all night to

Finding Fault

the Sangre de Cristo mountains and watch dawn flood the peaks with the color of Precious Blood, and we'll be married in Santa Fe." The nerve. Waiting for a sign from God indeed.

But you *are* drunk on this spectacular morning, drunk on love of your wife and children, on the impossible promise of the Resurrection, on this giddy Magritte canvas you seem to be walking through . . . drunk, perhaps, on Easter. You imagine—or do you in fact glimpse for a second?—the new creation. Even in your own memory, for crying out loud. You imagine your own life bereft of sin, which is conquered once and for all, after all.

Which leaves only good stuff from your childhood to behold and revere: The dance of dustmotes when somebody walked through a sunbeam near your playpen; the softness of your mother's hand on your cheek and forehead when you were tucked in at night; the intimate scratch of your father's whiskery cheek against your own when he would return from work; the music of cicadas and yellow light from the kitchen in the backyard on a summer night; fireflies, the smells of incense, candlewax and books; the eyes and eyelashes and lips and smell of the hair of the first girl you ever kissed. And so forth and so on: only what is most generous in your marriage, and only what is most blessed in your family, and only what is grandest in your own heart, and only the truest friends and happiest meetings and all of this appropriately and gratefully enwombed in the created and newly perfect universe;

and all of it contiguous with this great thing God is saying to nothing at all, for his own good reason or for no reason at all other than that he loves to say it; loves to say a word, to say The Word, come to think of it. The Word made flesh, bone, part and parcel of this whole and suddenly happy world.

So saturated with all that sheer and unearned happiness, you find yourself practically drowning in what your parochial grade school's nuns used to call Actual Grace. You remember: back in the days before burlap banners and the slide shows about waterfalls and wheat, Catholic grade school teachers used words like "grace." Actual Grace was this wonderful earthy stuff, like the wine at Cana, which could prime the pump, so to speak, for Sanctifying Grace, which, it was promised, could slake your thirst forever. All right, so it might not have been the best pedagogy, but what little kid in his or her right mind doesn't like to name things? Actual Grace, you'd been taught, could seep into this splendid sort of morning on which you presume upon the Son of the Most High.

And what happens then? What do you encounter on this new road to Emmaus, Indiana? A dead possum is what you encounter, and what you probably deserve for not leaving well enough alone. Zipadeedoo-dah this, Jack.

Dead? Hey, we are talking classic Midwestern road-burger here. It is quite possibly the corpse of that same oafish and slow moving mammal which had so amused

Finding Fault

your kids when they'd spotted it in the backyard a few mornings before. Dead isn't even the word for what this formerly entertaining critter is. If the Pogo before you is, as they say, playing possum, you are absolutely taken in. The tire treads and crows have pretty much finished their work, and now determined and voracious rivulets of ants are invading the grey carcass from all sides, like frenzied commuters streaming into an unpleasant city. Some nasty interior concentration of these, or perhaps a single, larger scavenger you'd just as soon not imagine at the moment, is causing the midsection to roll hideously. Gnats hover above the excavated eye sockets, eager for some disgusting nectar.

You quit whistling Zipadeedoodah as you bypass this grim harvesting. You'd been thinking about Easter and new life and red robins and hosts of golden daffodils and now the only thing rising in these parts is your gorge. Sobering thought that each one of those enthusiastically eviscerating bugs feels every bit at home in this morning, every bit as full of life and pep as you did a few moments ago. Hi ho, hi ho, it's in to work they go.

You're upwind as you pass by, so you're spared the brunt of the stench. Nevertheless, what you involuntarily whiff is pretty amazing. A few days ago, you read a letter from a friend in El Salvador who had photographed the exhumation of a death squad victim. For days afterward he'd been washing as frantically as

Michael O. Garvey

Lady Macbeth, convinced that the carrion redolence had become a part of him. Had Joseph of Arimathaea's tomb begun to smell like that inside before the stone was rolled away? Could be. You don't see icons of the Resurrection, they say, because it is an event which is literally unimaginable. You can barely imagine the physical restoration of this rotting chunk of possum meat, let alone the overthrowing of death. It's a long way from putrefaction to outright glory. From this atrocious roadburger odor to the aroma of freshly caught fish grilling on a charcoal fire on the shore of the Sea of Tiberias. From a discouraging fishing expedition to a picnic with God. All he had to say was come and get it, boys, and they knew right away who was cooking their breakfast.

There is a sort of bashfulness about the contemporary manner in which folks speak of the Resurrection. Among learned believers from Rome to Berkeley, you hear Jesus' rising described in utterly abstract theological gobbledegook instead of clear (if somewhat startled) English. There is an apparent reluctance to say or think it in the stark terms this bizarre occurrence seems to require: that Jesus had been a dead man in a dead man's body—a thing that would gross you right out of existence just as does this squished possum here, and that he has been seen alive, in a live man's body, his own body. Himself. And that he might show up anywhere at all, even in Rome or Berkeley. And that he might come upon your own dead self anytime at all— fishing in the Sea of Tiberias, whistling Zipadeedoo-

Finding Fault

dah on some Indiana road, or nearly losing your breakfast on account of a flattened possum. And that no pile of maggot-infested flesh, no ingrown and diseased mind, no cowardly heart or suffocating soul is safe from the joy he comes to inflict.

Compared with that joy, you guess that even a dazzling morning like this one doesn't add up to a whole lot more than a heap of dead possum. Why search among the dead for one who lives? He is risen even as he said. What an amazing religion.

Not that this morning is all that bad a thing. That hideous roadburger ennobles the life abounding all around, and the whole glorious morning is made to rise up and surround it. Besides, on this stage of the journey home to the new Jerusalem, you have to take your dead possums with your live ones, the stink of death with the induplicable smell of a newborn baby's scalp, and, of course, sin with mercy.

Hey, speaking of sin, Sinner, you got yourself a job to go to. Your gut has pretty much evened itself out by now, and the morning sun is slapping you on the back like a boozy alumnus at reunion time. Up the road apiece, a golden retriever scampers back and forth on a dew-spangled lawn, barking endlessly and idiotically. Damn dog looks for all the world like it's laughing at you, and you yourself feel suddenly like laughing out loud. What must this scene look like to some little kid, for instance, looking out from inside a passing car while his mom and dad are arguing about bills? Here's a man and a dog laughing and barking at each

Michael O. Garvey

other. What must it . . . what does it . . . look like to
the risen Lord? This might be among the many things
they must mean when they say alleluia.

You don't say alleluia just then, but you do resume
whistling Zipadeedoodah. Same difference, you suppose.

St. Gabriel, Patron of the NRA?

O N OUR front porch, in a little glass bowl filled with blue gravel and smelly water, there once lived a newt named Bronto—so named because the newt's master, a six-year-old whose parents had refused him permission to adopt a more mammalian pet, had observed that his newt looked a little like the Brontosaurus in his favorite reference book. Bronto was not what you would call fleet of foot. In fact, Bronto was so sedentary that I am still not entirely persuaded that Bronto was ever alive, which, now that I think about it, would account for the way the water in his bowl smelled as well as for the fact that his six-year-old master had lost all interest in him by the time his mother (the master's mother, not Bronto's) one morning flushed the poor reptile down the toilet in a fit of abstraction, but I digress.

I thought about Bronto one morning while reading a report on the efforts of a group called the Citizens Committee to Keep and Bear Arms to have the Vatican declare Saint Gabriel Possenti the patron saint of handgunners. According to John M. Snyder, chief flack for these gun freaks, Saint Gabriel, a Passionist priest from the previous century, once prevented the rape of a young Italian woman by an act of intimidation worthy of Dirty Harry, seizing a handgun from one of her abductors and blowing away a nearby liz-

Michael O. Garvey

ard "with one shot." Saint Gabriel thus demonstrated, said Mr. Snyder, "that an individual committed in heart, mind and soul to almighty God can use an instrument to bring about practical good here on earth." Go ahead, Bronto. Make my day!

The United States Catholic Conference, whose staff sometimes seem bent on proving that humorlessness is the central charism of their ministry, had let it be known that the designation of a patron saint for handgunners would conflict with attitudes expressed in the Conference's earlier statements (You know, those statements incessantly quoted in all the debates) on handgun control. It would be interesting . . . all right, not interesting, but pertinent, to review past statements of the USCC on mental illness, to see if the impact of these was similarly diminished by the designation of Saint Dymphna as the patroness of the insane, but again I digress.

I was all for a patron saint for handgunners and frankly couldn't understand why the bureaucrats of the USCC were opposed to such a harmless notion. The only reasonable objection to what these gun-toting hooples were requesting was that it had been granted already. In his indispensable *The Catholic Fact Book* (Thomas More Press, $23.95), John Deedy listed Saint Barbara, a 3rd-century virgin and martyr, as the approved patroness of "artillerymen" and "gunners," categories which surely include petitioners ranging from eccentric blunderbuss collectors to undersexed survivalists. Saint Barbara got associated

Finding Fault

with artillerypersons shortly after she'd been imprisoned, tortured and beheaded for being a Christian. Her pagan father, Dioscorus, who had carried out the death sentence was struck by lightning and consumed entirely. Saint Barbara, according to my grandfather's edition of the Catholic Encyclopedia, is also protectress of people threatened by thunderstorms and fire. I couldn't imagine why she wouldn't intercede for all of us hopeless and vulnerable pudknockers who were trying to be kind and sane, maintaining marriages and raising children in these last weird moments before a few decisive strategists set nuclear fire to the earth. But that was an awful large cargo of souls for a solitary 3rd-century virgin and martyr to be interceding for.

So why not relieve Saint Barbara of a few million clients? Why not designate a patron or patroness for those equally troubled folk who, like our former first lady, felt a need to keep a little bitty (or did she say teeny weeny?) hand gun by their bedsides? There were patron saints for advertising executives, motorcyclists, funeral directors, notaries, mailmen and airline stewardesses (no *not* letter carriers and flight attendants . . . designators of patron saints don't goof around with gender inclusion . . . although there may well be a patron saint of gender inclusion), so why not a patron saint for those Butch-Waxed, flat-topped sociopaths who liked to relieve the tedium of their lives by slipping on the combat fatigues, grabbing a wine cooler or two from the icebox, holing up in the garage with a few back issues of *Soldier of Fortune*, and fiddling around with the old .357 mag? Of all the Church's members, these folks deserved to know that someone keeps watch over them. And the rest of us deserved to know that this someone was sanctified, well armed, and a very good shot.

Which led me to part ways with my brothers and sisters—if sisters are allowed within the sandbagged perimeter—on the Citizens Committee to Keep and Bear Firearms. Either Saint Gabriel Possenti was the wrong intercessor for this job, or Mr. Snyder was an incompetent publicist and should have asked his patroness, Saint Bernardine of Siena for guidance. If the lizard bagged by Saint Gabriel a century ago was anything like Bronto the Newt in the bowl on our front porch, there was nothing very impressive about the saint's marksmanship. To begin with, Saint Gabriel would have been shooting at a pretty much stationary target. I'm no Oliver North, and I knew it was no challenge to hit Bronto from fifteen feet away with a casually aimed rubber band. With a handgun, it would have been, if not like shooting fish in a barrel, at least like shooting lizards in a bowl. Easier, in fact, because fish move faster than lizards. Lots faster if newts may be said to represent the average lizard's potential velocity. Had the target been a cat, the kill would have been something to brag about. Three cats lived two doors down from us and frequently made unauthorized use of the sandbox in our backyard. Even after three years of assiduous brickbat flinging, often at very close range, neither my boys nor I had so

Finding Fault

much as stunned one of the damned things, but yet again I digress.

Another thing: What made Mr. Snyder so breezily confident that Saint Gabriel's one shot killed that barely mobile lizard anyway? An argument was once raging in our house, or would have been, had anyone cared, about whether or not the lizard in the smelly bowl on our front porch was alive. The lizard in Mr. Snyder's story might have been missed by the shot and had the presence of mind to play possum, patiently awaiting a ceasefire and stealing away after rapists, rescued and rescuers had withdrawn from this edifying scene. Was Mr. Snyder willing to risk the celestial entrenchment of some geek who couldn't hit a newt with a rubber band in an office which handles the petitions of combat-decorated, by-God marksmen?

With all due respect to the Citizens Committee to Keep and Bear Firearms, it seemed to me that we should, for now, leave this particular slot unfilled. At least until the certified snipers of the Church could propose a more impressive candidate. In the meantime, I figured we should commend the staffmembers of the USCC who so gravely opposed them to the loving protection of St. Vitus, patron of comedians, who may have enabled them to take themselves a bit less seriously.

Leaving the Causeway

"The law is not a 'light' for you or any man to see by; the law is not an instrument of any kind. The law is a causeway upon which, so long as he keeps to it, a citizen may walk safely . . . In matters of conscience, the loyal subject is more bounden to be loyal to his conscience than to any other thing."

WHEN Robert Bolt wrote *A Man For All Seasons*, he relied heavily on English court records for some of Saint Thomas More's most eloquent speeches. The eloquence, the insight and the man all came to mind during the last few dog days when word came that a federal court in Norfolk, Virginia, has passed sentence on Philip Berrigan and three other representatives of the Plowshares group.

Berrigan received the maximum six-month sentence for doing some minor damage to the U.S.S. Iowa's cruise missile launchers, wacking at them with hammer and boltcutters and splattering some blood. Sister Margaret McKenna received a suspended sentence; Gregory Boertje got six months and Andrew Lawrence four.

With equal measures of diffidence and respect, I confess that such actions manage to miss my head and thus my heart as well. Confronted with the Plow-

Finding Fault

sharers large and risky deed, I begin to feel like George Bush at a Grateful Dead concert. I don't "get" it. I think I understand the horror it points to; I think I understand the implicit intention to break the death-trance we all seem to be locked in; I think I even see, though through a glass darkly, that the pouring of blood has to do with redemption, awakening, and new life. It's easier for me to understand the closely related civilly disobedient work of the participants in Operation Rescue, who simply surround abortion clinics and make their smooth running impossible. I know many people who have made and suffered for making such gestures. Among them is one of the kindest people I've ever met, and among them is one of the most destructively selfish people I've ever met. They are, like people who work for the Pentagon, a mixed group. I envy them their clarity, and I wish I could see in their work the polar opposite of the death so efficiently produced and sold by the abortion industry and the Pentagon. I can't.

But they sure do have the relationship between law and conscience compellingly displayed. Whatever their motives, they clearly have been willing to slip off the safe causeway for a bit, and to walk along a somewhat more dangerous path. Six months of anything is a long time. Six months for a 64-year-old man is longer. Six months of jail is an enormity. Philip Berrigan's close familiarity with the menace, precarity and tedium of prison life makes impressive and gener-

Michael O. Garvey

ous his apparent readiness to endure this much more of it. Whatever else might be missed by us dullards, it's easy to "get" the bravery.

In brother Daniel Berrigan's autobiography, *To Dwell In Peace*, one gets the bravery, too. Banged around in the early reviews, the book is an anomalous a piece of work as its author, a delightful man of—well, there's no way around the word—disarming personality who has for the last quarter of a century entertained, infuriated and enlightened just about everybody who pays attention to anything. A sad and scary childhood, Jesuit bootcamp, the slings and arrows of outrageous ecclesial rectitude, the fatuities of the academy and the enigmas of his celebrity are all done up here in Fr. Berrigan's distinctive voice. In the finest chapter, as he writes about his present and impressive ministry among New York AIDS victims, he remembers the unabashedly homosexual prisoners he'd seen quarantined from the general population of the federal prison in Danbury during one of his several captivities. In their flamboyant defiance of the customary institutional ways of making do, Fr. Berrigan saw these men "staging a drama of absurdity and redemption, for the benefit of some and the fury of others." Such theatrics have always received and will always receive widely diverse reviews, from my own "Gee, I dunno" to the more spirited calls for rack and rope.

But these dramas are always arresting, and not only for the actors in them. Like St. Thomas More, the Berrigans and Plowshare folk, Joan Andrews and the

Finding Fault

hundreds of Operation Rescue people are treasures of the Church. They seize the imagination for a moment and invite consideration of events on the larger landscape through which the legal causeway winds, a place dotted with names like Eden, Bethlehem, Gethsemani, Golgotha, Emmaus, and Paradise, a universe enormous and strange—indifferent to that strip of familiarity and custom which sometimes seems so solid and sure that we're tempted to mistake it for sacred. Thank God for them.

The Fruit of Limbo

AFTER bedtime prayers, Joseph Benedict, age four, asks whether his stuffed animals, Buzzer the Rabbit, Grumpy the Bear, and Gorilla the Blue Gorilla, will be allowed to accompany him to heaven. His father was not trained by wily Dominican nuns for nothing and answers readily: God knows you and loves you and wants you to be happy forever with him. If you need Buzzer, Grumpy and Gorilla to make you happy forever with God, then you bet they'll come to him with you.

The ingenuous face that looks up from the crowded pillow cautiously accepts the theological principle. But only cautiously. Joseph has already been in the church for four years, long enough to understand what a tricky thing God's love can be. God, after all, is stronger (and so, scarier) than Hulk Hogan. God's love, he already knows, has something to do with the woman Mary and her special baby Jesus, and with the defiant coziness of a crowded stable against a chilly Christmas night, and with wise and kindly Oriental visitors bringing exotic gifts to an uncomprehending little boy, and also with the shattered and bloody corpse nailed to a tree whose image hangs on the living room wall as if Joseph's parents weren't frightened by it. About Buzzer, Grumpy and Gorilla, he can be more confident. They are not fierce and he will not need to

Finding Fault

search for them. Even in the teeth of God's love, they are predictable, familiar and friendly. He crushes Buzzer against his cheek, closes his eyes and that's that.

His father is momentarily pleased by the benevolent craftiness of the answer he's given. Lesser parents might have begun playing around with phenomenological distinctions or bizarre analyses of the spirit/ body dichotomy or, worse, ignored the question. He, on the other hand, has protected the integrity of his son's childhood, for another few weeks anyway, and that is a more challenging task in these horrible times than most people realize. To think of the middle-class peeves you read about in Catholic newspapers (priestly celibacy, the role of women in the church, *Humanae Vitae*) when this is the *real* stuff, the stuff about which people are *really* worried. The idea of stuffed animals in heaven. Cute. But how cute? How much more mature is his own notion of heaven? What hope, if any, underwrites his bothering to pass this stuff on to his son as his parents passed it on to him and theirs to them?

It gets him thinking. Life after death. Resurrection. These things had sure as hell better be real. And more real than that pale stuff reflected in glib assertions like "Oscar Romero lives on in the hearts of the Salvadoran people." (He's dead, in other words.) What is there after the lungs no longer take air, the heart no longer pumps, the senses drop off one by one and the relentless materiality of the universe closes in? May a person

147

hope in a heaven, with or without stuffed animals, after all? What about all that Elizabeth Kübler-Ross stuff—people anticipating great journeys, rough feelings of being borne aloft, drawing near the smiling faces of one's dearest lost loved ones? Those reassurances are our own stuffed animals.

He remembers first hearing about the beatific vision, a theological truth whose strange name provoked in his first-grade imagination something like the NBC-TV peacock. The thought of staring at that strange bird forever struck fear, not joy, into his heart. The thought of staring at anything for eternity, even the face of God, seemed horrible to him. The thought of *anything* for eternity, the thought of eternity itself, that seamless and unyielding enormity, afflicted him with nausea.

And he remembers thinking that there was a certain injustice inherent in the notion, too. His baptism as a Catholic (he knew with a savage certainty in those simpler pre-conciliar days) consigned him to one of two distinctly unappetizing fates: eternal hellfire or temporary purgative horror followed by endless beatific vision. He remembers envying the decent, ordinary, unbaptized folk who went to limbo, the place that, in his imagination at least, was really heaven. The good public school kids who had escaped baptisms of desire and blood, the kids who didn't commit mortal sins and who muddled their bovine, pagan ways through life would, he knew, go to limbo, that place the Dominican sisters had assured him was ex-

Finding Fault

actly like the earth, only nobody died or got sick and everyone was happy all the time.

If only he hadn't been baptized.

If only God had never intervened at all! The ferocity of the thought and the unwilled blasphemy startle him now. Looking at his sleeping son, he feels a rush of rage and sorrow. Why must he and now his poor boy, too, be doomed to a steadfast refusal to come to terms?

Called forth from nothingness, they have been cast on alien soil to live in humiliation as exiles from an unseen homeland. They will pay this earth its rent, spending on its history their pity, humility and forebearance. They will try to be good tenants in the kingdom of blood and dung and necessity. But they will always be aliens there, perpetually unhappy, perpetually vulnerable, perpetually insecure. They will never be satisfied. They will never taste the fruit of limbo.

The Catholic Worker at Fifty

IN MEL PIEHL'S excellent history, *Breaking Bread*, it is described by a rich and compact phrase: "a movement of utopian dissent." And the reasons for the dissent are manifold. A society in which infanticide and genocide are casually discussed on the Donahue television show; in which fatuity and selfishness are looked upon as virtues; in which entire aisles of supermarkets are devoted to pet foods; in which the distinctions between liturgy and therapy become obscure—that society is sound asleep. It awaits the coming of Christ in much the same spirit a drunk driver awaits an oncoming Mack truck in the wrong lane: any stirring is potentially fruitful, even if it's not necessarily enough to avoid the disaster.

People I know who have been or are now associated with the Catholic Worker have this in common: a strong sense that our customary ways of making do simply won't do; a profound suspicion that most allegiances to the state are idolatrous; and a belief that things do not have to be the way they are. Those people have little else in common, and among them are some of the kindest, strangest, most self-pitying and self-righteous, most courageous, most and least saintly, funniest, most interesting and most boring people I've ever met.

150

Finding Fault

Fear, charity, conviction, tedium and holiness drive people to these soup kitchens and houses of hospitality and to the steps of the Pentagon and the arms bazaars. What they do in those places is done in the name of Jesus, or because people they admire have invited them, or because their marriages are failing, or because they love their children, or because they believe their actions please God. They are the twitches in a paralyzed limb; insomniacs in an otherwise silent dormitory.

All of us who are or have been associated with the Catholic Worker phenomenon would agree with Francois Mauriac that "political wisdom is not separated from that wisdom which was taught from the Mount. When the meek were promised that they would possess the earth and those who thirst after justice that they will have their fill, this promise was also addressed to the nations of the world."

When communities of men and women attempt to respond to that promise, they last for a few weeks or for fifty years. As in marriages, people grow strong together or inflict terrible damage on each other, or become passive-aggressive or just plain aggressive, or show each other the face of Christ or show each other a most hideous face, or separate and go their different and baffled ways.

And the communities lurch along, those that survive, from folly to triumph to disaster to relief and to triumph again. It is a peculiarly Catholic phenome-

Michael O. Garvey

non: a sinful collective which gives a feeble witness and encounters grace. It gave me my closest friends and my wife. How can I be objective about it?

Here in South Bend, from the late-night, long-distance phone calls we receive and from the gossip of visiting friends, we get the impression that the only substantial threat to the Catholic Worker movement is that nuclear war it so assiduously opposes. People still extend hospitality to poor strangers, still complain about the burdens of community life, still refuse to pay war taxes, still go over the fence at the Strategic Air Command, still distribute leaflets to workers in defense industry plants.

And they still tell stories about friends: Jeff and Catherine in Los Angeles, and Tom and Monica in Waterbury, and how Sonny Cordaro is in/out of jail; how Karl Meyer is leading tax resister chorales in the Chicago post office; what's new in Alderson; what somebody heard about what was new at 36 East First St. in New York. I wonder if the Catholic Worker confederacy (of which we see only a fraction) was ever more firmly cemented. I wonder if it ever will be.

What is most to be honored in the Catholic Worker movement in its 50th anniversary is its wildness, its witness to the fact that at the heart of the Christian life there is something dazzling and unpredictable. For fifty years its vagabond membership has pointed toward a truth which Peter Maurin called "the dynamite of the church." The charge lay undetonated in 1933 and remains undetonated today; most attempts to do-

Finding Fault

mesticate Mother Church are heartbreakingly effective.

But as long as the movement survives, there will be a few public examples of the sporadic and occasionally laughable impulse to live a life which, without the gospel, would be senseless. And there will be a few people who insist that the Church not sit down quietly among other institutions. There will be a few supercilious misfits, too, eager to use their radicalism as a stick with which to beat the ghosts of their adolescence. Disorder is the price of exuberance.

In an age so keen to subdue the church, it is a price worth paying.

The Ambassador Goes To Church

O N SUNDAY mornings when he was United States Ambassador to El Salvador, Edwin G. Corr used to attend the Union Church, a nondenominational institution at the end of Calle 4 in Colonia La Mascota, one of the pleasant and affluent neighborhoods which crowd the extreme western section of San Salvador. The city's wealthy have traditionally occupied this area which geological accident has left least susceptible to the dangers of earthquake.

The Union Church, regularly visited by many members of the swelling community of U.S. employees and agents in El Salvador, is oddly located: Calle 4, like the affluence flanking it, ends abruptly at the church entrance, giving way to a dirt footpath which leads into the squalor and chaos of Mascota No. 1, a large cluster of fragile shacks populated by dogs, rats, chickens, and families, most of them late arrivals, who have been displaced both by the army's scorched-earth operations against the F.M.L.N. guerrillas and the massive earthquake which struck the capital city in the fall of 1986. While 600,000 people have already fled El Salvador, there are still at least a half million of these less fortunate *desplezados*, displaced people, within the tiny country's borders.

"Displaced" is an adjective which seems insufficient to describe the vulnerability of more than a fourth of

Finding Fault

El Salvador's families, the precarity of their survival and the horror of their everyday plight. Victims of a purposeful military strategy intended to isolate the guerrillas from the potential support of the *masas*, the masses, they are driven before the hemisphere's most relentless army to become *desplezados*. El Salvador's nearly psychedelic military and bureaucratic jargon accuses them, because to be one of the *desplazados* means that one may also be said to belong to the *masas*, and to belong to the *masas* is to be associated, in the minds of the powerful, with the guerrillas. Nobody wants to be one of the *masas*. The wording of army memoranda indicates a particularly violent animosity toward the *masas*, and while there is no clear definition of the term there is no escape from the category either. Many such people live close by the church at the end of Calle 4.

Mascota No. 1 is really something to see, especially if you are a *gringo* tourist unused to the overwhelming and nearly universal poverty of El Salvador.

The neighborhood is noisy with the chatter and laughter of brown-eyed kids with swollen, malnourished and worm-infested bellies. They flash shy smiles at you split seconds before their faces disappear into the folds of their mother's dresses. Their mothers are more grave, speaking less and quietly, leaning gracefully against empty doorframes of unlit homes from which waft the smells of woodsmoke, burnt cornmeal, and urine. From time to time their grandmothers call softly from hammocks inside the shacks, sometimes

155

scolding the mischievous, sometimes wanting to know about the intentions of those *gringos* outside. As you walk deeper into the neighborhood, you become an involuntary Pied Piper for whole processions of these abused and charming little kids, hopping from bank to bank of the haphazard canal which serves as the community's sewer.

Ambassador Coor's arrival at the Union Church used to be something to see, too, especially if you were a *gringo* tourist out on an aimless stroll and unused to the rhythms of contemporary Salvadoran life. The normally sleepy street would seem to explode. A variegated fleet of brand new Japanese cars and vans would roar past, shriek to a tire-shredding standstill at the entrances of the church and the slum, and disgorge into the ensuing cumulus clouds of dust and rubber smoke at least a dozen and a half fast-moving, sunglass-bespectacled, submachine gun-toting embassy bodyguards, most of whom would bark incomprehensible instructions into their walkie-talkies as they fanned out into the slum, up the forested hill beside the church, and along Calle 4's sidewalks, curbs and driveway entrances. At some point during this invasion and occupation, Ambassador Corr would go up to the house of the Lord.

The apprehensions of the embassy security people were certainly justifiable. The guerrilla soldiers of the F.M.L.N. have several times in recent years demonstrated the ease with which they can strike pretty much anywhere and against pretty much anyone in the

Finding Fault

country. Were the thickets above the Union Church or the slum which sweeps up to it left unguarded, it would not be very difficult for persons so inclined and equipped to assault the church during the ambassador's weekly visit. So Sunday in and Sunday out, the logic of war, the liturgical customs of Christianity, and Mr. Corr's religious preference all being what they were, the neighborhood of the Ambassador's church must be invaded, occupied and made safe for Mr. Corr's arrival.

It was soon, the rumor went, to be made even safer. The residents of the slum at the end of Calle 4 had lately been visited by technical looking men with surveying instruments. These gentlemen had brought them to understand that the embassy's security people had assessed the ambassador's weekly schedule and determined that the moment when Mr. Corr was at greatest risk was the time he set aside for Sunday worship. The security people were uneasy about the dead end of Calle 4. Thinking it unwise for such an attractive target to spend such a predictable amount of time in such a strategically vulnerable spot, they had decided that a safe route must be established to provide an emergency exit from the Union Church and quick access to the Paseo Escalon, the main street in the area. And the route which they had proposed ran directly through Mascota No. 1.

Because the present arrangement was intolerably dangerous, somebody's routine would have to be changed, and the poorest of the neighborhood's resi-

157

dents suspected that it was unlikely to be the ambassador's. This hallucinatory collision between American convenience and Salvadoran livelihood was only one irony in a country whose entire history seems to have been written by a cynical humorist.

I never found out how this minor subplot in the larger tragedy of El Salvador was resolved. Admittedly, it was heartening to learn that the Ambassador was willing to put himself at considerable risk in order to celebrate the Lord's day. But how could the Ambassador safely worship in the manner to which he was accustomed without demolishing at least a few hundred precarious homes of the hemisphere's most abused and already twice-displaced families?

It is a sin to judge a man, and no one but God alone dare measure the integrity of Edwin Corr's prayers, but it certainly seemed forgiveable, and perhaps even obligatory, to share the bewilderment voiced by one exasperated grandmother whose home was among the many impeding the potential escape route from the Union Church to the Paseo Escalon: "God knows what God the man prays to!"

In Santa Cruz

From six in the evening until six in the morning they enforce a strict curfew. We are not allowed to leave our houses, and they come into our homes and take them over as if they were theirs. They steal our firewood, our beans, and our corn; whatever they can take from us to eat. And we're all afraid to say anything, because we don't want to provoke their anger. Some of our people say they wouldn't mind if the soldiers just took a little corn, but what happens is that 200 soldiers come in and stay from 2 weeks to a month, or even a month and a half. Every day they take things—they mess up the work that has been done, and they leave the people frightened from all the shooting that goes on day and night in the vicinity.

S O TWO Salvadoran friends had written in a letter from their village. It had been my graced fortune to spend Easter with them there a few months earlier.

Santa Cruz, in Usulutan, El Salvador, is a tiny community of astonishingly vulnerable people, *desplezados*, those people displaced by the war who now make up nearly a quarter of El Salvador's population. It lies in the middle of what the Salvadoran army calls a conflictive zone, a region which neither the army nor the guerrillas have been able to control. Most of its res-

Michael O. Garvey

idents have fled there from even more frightening places; many of its residents have lost whole families to the routine butchery that is contemporary Salvadoran life; and all of its residents are tired of running.

The village sprawls along a low mountain spur, a haphazard arrangement of ramshackle huts, crudely constructed of forked stakes and palm thatch, roofed, when the builders have been fortunate, with scraps of moulded aluminum. Many of these structures line the parched creekbed which creases the spur's northern edge, sloping downward to become a footpath to a tributary of the nearby Rio Lempa, the sole source of the village's water. A round trip between Santa Cruz and water takes two and a half hours, and during the six-month-long dry season, an able-bodied resident of the village, no matter what age or gender, must expect to make it twice, unless he is fortunate enough to have a pack animal. The most appropriate times for this journey are the cooler periods of the day, around sunrise and sunset, but the path is treacherous, steep, and invisible in the very early morning, when villagers need to carry flashlights with them. Ray-o-Vac batteries are precious in Santa Cruz.

The downhill walk is a dusty, sweaty and unpleasant affair, and the return trip nullifies the fleeting refreshment of the villagers' daily bath. People in Santa Cruz nevertheless endure this trek not only for their survival, but also for the dignity lent by clean clothes and the pleasure of feeling human a few minutes each

Finding Fault

morning. In contrast to the gritty exposure of their living quarters, their watering place is a cool, green haven where the volume of conversation, with abrupt reverence, drops below that of the softly running water in which they launder and bathe.

The C-ration cans littering the road by which some North American friends and I first approached the village indicated that soldiers from the nearby military garrison at Usulutan had been in Santa Cruz quite recently. Confirming this, the villagers who greeted us seemed pleased to have "internationals" visiting. It was possible, my friends and I were told, that the presence of witnesses with foreign passports might incline the soldiers to abuse the villagers less than usual.

It was pleasant for us, if disconcerting, to carry this pathetic gift, a modicum of possible relief, with us. Our other presents for the people of Santa Cruz were two pinatas stuffed with rock candy, to be shattered by the town's children after the Easter Mass, and a priest to celebrate it and baptize the village children. For free. Nearly forty baptisms took place that Easter.

Any priest, let alone this *gringo* who would baptize their children for free, was a novelty for these folks. The nearest parish, in Berlin, is a four-hour walk up this same hopelessly unpaved road through harsh and mountainous terrain contested by the Salvadoran army and the F.M.L.N. The parish priest in Berlin seemed to be a kind, but troubled and easily intimidated man. He emphasized his reluctance to make this

161

journey by insisting that the impoverished villagers pay five colons (slightly more than a dollar then) apiece for baptisms. He had been pleased, nevertheless, to know that we would visit the village, and, whether in a spirit of hospitality or of guilt, had given us dinner in a local diner and a place to sleep in his house the night before. But such pastoral care as was available to the people of Santa Cruz must be extended by laypeople bereft of institutional Church commission.

"Traditional autocrats," wrote Jeanne Kirkpatrick in the chillingly patrician and now-famous 1979 *Commentary* article which launched her political career, "do not disturb the habitual rhythms of work and leisure, habitual places of residence, habitual patterns of family and personal relations. Because the miseries of traditional life are familiar, they are bearable to ordinary people who, growing up in the society, learn to cope, as children born to untouchables in India acquire the skills and attitudes necessary for survival in the miserable roles they are destined to fill. Such societies create no refugees."

Her remarks seem poignant, even ludicrous, in relation to Santa Cruz, a community made up entirely of refugees, where the diurnal rhythms of misery are disrupted only when the Salvadoran army accelerates them. Otherwise, the traditional life of these landless folks remain undisturbed by the powerful. They learn to slake their thirst, keep clean, deal with their sewage, and scrape together a subsistence living free from such

Finding Fault

governmental intrusions as electricity or water proj-
ects, rudimentary schooling, or the protection of law.

It hurts so much whenever we think about it, my
Salvadoran friends had written, *but we must tell you
that a horrible thing happened recently in Santa Cruz.
An older man by the name of Pilar, who was 60 years
old, was killed in his house July 11. He was machine-
gunned as he lay in his hammock sleeping at night.
Soldiers of the Sixth Infantry Brigade in Usulutan
killed him, and they did it only because he refused to
sell them bread. Pilar had gone all the way to Berlin to
buy the bread for a neighbor woman. This killing was
a cold-blooded, premeditated act on the part of the
soldiers, and we have denounced it accordingly as
strongly as we could. But here's the problem: terrible
things like this happen without anyone finding out
about it, so the soldiers go unpunished. You and other
people in your community could be of great assistance
in denouncing crimes like this, to help defend our
physical security, and to help assure our right to live
out here where we do.*

This modest suggestion engendered several telephone calls, telex messages and letters to the American
Embassy, to Napoleon Duarte, who was then titular
president of the country, and to various Salvadoran
military officials. The result, I discovered during a
later visit, was the closest approximation of justice
that people of Santa Cruz may reasonably expect: The
soldiers responsible for the murder of an innocent old

163

Michael O. Garvey

man were transferred to another command, and the lieutenant in charge of them was administered a slap on the wrist.

The people I met in Santa Cruz were, like these two friends, profoundly unrealistic. Drawing from their shared squalor they proffered regal hospitality, affectionately solicitous of their *gringo* guests. On Holy Saturday night, speaking hopefully about the future of their children, they had paused to gauge the distance of one alarmingly audible bombing and resumed their enthusiastic observations without comment the instant the earth stopped shaking. At Easter Mass, one of them had preached cheerfully about the signs of Christ's presence in this precarious place where the refusal of the local clergy to visit starves the people of eucharistic bread, where children regularly see their mothers and sisters harassed and molested by local soldiers, and where parents watch helplessly as the bellies of their babies swell with intestinal parasites.

On my second visit to Santa Cruz, I witnessed several more "free" baptisms. I particularly remember the twin boys of a beaming man named Silverio, in whose house I stayed. I recently learned that Silverio's babies died at eighteen months of age within a few days of each other, of diarrhea. This could have been treated with a few cents worth of Pepto Bismol, but the Salvadoran Army will not permit any medicines to reach Santa Cruz, because it is within guerrilla territory and its residents are therefore considered guerrillas. There is a perverse accuracy to the logic, I suppose. Had

Finding Fault

those babies been allowed to grow to manhood in bloody Usulutan, they very well may have become guerrillas in that seemingly endless war which rages unnoticed by its primary sponsors to the north.

The victimized people of Santa Cruz certainly know that in the social rubble and human carnage of contemporary life, the military's nonchalant murder of one old peasant and the killing of innocent children are barely noticeable things, and yet they have the awesome temerity of all Christians. They have a wisdom not accessible to economic, political, military analysis. They know that their anguish is profoundly significant because it is the very anguish of Christ. They know also that we who surround the same Eucharist are their brothers and sisters, and that we are minimally obliged by virtue of their request to raise our voices in their behalf.

Santa Cruz is the merest fraction of misery in a country where atrocity is commonplace, and it is always unclear whether the letters of guilty liberals measurably influence anyone or anything there. What is quite clear is that the villagers regularly request that American friends write them. Like the gifts my friends and I took with us on our visit there a few months ago, knee-jerk letters of protest are feeble offerings which fall far short of what the people of Santa Cruz deserve. But feeble as they are, they are offerings we alone can give to these suffering *desplezados* who are, in Christ, flesh of our flesh, bone of our bone, Eucharist of our Eucharist.

Help from Rome

S O MUCH in the Church and the world is heart-breaking, infuriating, confusing, and distracting. But on occasion, almost as if to prove that Our Lord has a sense of humor, his spouse, our Church, provides us with something to laugh about.

On income tax day, while U.S. Christians agonized about the degrees of intimacy in their friendship with the mammon of iniquity, while some paid taxes and others resisted, while not much was going on in the liturgical life of the Church (the feast of Easter's renewing warmth still spread, but it was a ferial day), the Vatican issued one hell of a funny decree.

It came from a pontifical commission (for migration and tourism), which probably has an office next to Sister Annunciata's broom closet, and concerns itself with faculties for chaplains authorized for ministry to migrants and (I'm not making this up) "nomads, circus troupes and traveling businessmen and women, to those who work in airports and on airplanes, as well as to the air navigators—pilots and passengers—to tourists and pilgrims for their entire duration of their charge." Only our Church would remember circus troupes.

Among the faculties granted, #3 ("to use electric lamps in place of candles when the mass is celebrated in the open or on board ships or planes if there are no

166

candles or they cannot be used") is my favorite. What if the deacon forgot to pack the Duracells? Quick, somebody call Rome! (Number seven is good, too.) If someone is dying, and as long as he or she is "properly prepared and disposed," the chaplain may administer the sacrament of confirmation. Somehow I find it difficult to imagine a fallen away Baptist breathing his last, converting to the Church and confronted by a priest who slaps him in the face and asks him what name he wants to choose from the litany before he'll absolve a single sin.

Among the privileges granted to the faithful in this decree, most of which concern plenary indulgences (remember plenary indulgences?) and the complicated ways that these may be obtained, #3 dispenses circus people, traveling businessmen and women and nomads (but not, presumably, seamen, navigators and tourists, who get all sorts of other stuff) "from the law on fast and abstinence contained in the apostolic constitution 'Paenitemini' (cf. III, II, 2, 3)." And it's high time, too. I've been burdened for years by that damn Pimatoony. It looms over every family vacation and has scourged the McDonald's empire.

According to Cardinal Sebastiano Baggio—the driving power behind the Migration and Tourism Commission, the man who makes the whole thing really work—Pope John Paul II "deigned to approve with his authority these faculties and privileges and ordered them to be published" back in December of last year. I wonder what took them so long?

Michael O. Garvey

Well, as a conservative Catholic, I'm happy to pledge my support to this decree. I solemnly promise never to abuse the privileges it bestows. I thank God daily that my parents brought me up in the same Church whose Pontifical Commission on Migration and Tourism next to Sister Annunciata's broom closet has published this curious document.

But I'll not take part in the stormy debate which will surely attend the promulgation of the decree. I mean, it freed the circus troupes from Pimatoony, didn't it? Let's be content with that.

The Ministry of Bitching

SOMEONE—Kingsley Amis, I think—said that everything that has gone wrong since World War II can be summed up by the word "workshop," but even that observation has become outdated. Holy Mother Zeitgeist has since inflicted worse wounds on our language and, in consequence, our lives.

Ordinarily bad-tempered, engagingly aggressive businessmen are no longer allowed to "tell" anybody anything. Now all males worthy of their testosterone must cry when they're told to, and they must "share." (As in "Let's share with Jim why we fired him." Or "Honey, I have something I want to share with you. I'm in love with our ostrich and I want a divorce.")

Mother Zeitgeist has drawn a bead on Mother-Church, too. Have you noticed lately that any activity (with the possible exceptions of embezzlement and rape) undertaken by Christians has become "ministry"?

The nice people who help distribute communion are, where I go to Mass, "ministers of the cup" or "cup ministers." The kind people who take unwed, distressed and pregnant young women into their families are ministers of hospitality (as are folks we called "ushers" in earlier days).

The good friend who comes to the aid of friends is told that he or she performs a valuable ministry. Hell,

169

Michael O. Garvey

we don't even know who our friends are these days. We can't invite folks over for a beer and a chat for fear that we'll wind up ministering to them or, worse, they to us. I wonder whether we can even fall in love as long as we're in ministry's teeth.

Everyone's ministering to everyone else. Doesn't anyone do favors anymore? I was complaining about these things the other night as I sat on our front porch with a friend. As he left, he thanked me for my ministry of bitching.

I'm not sure how this ministry business got a foothold in our vineyard. When I was a little boy, "ministers" were those scrubbed-looking men with big Adam's apples and deep voices and phony Southern accents who talked about "Gawd" and "Jeesuss" from the pulpits of the small-altared churches into which, we assumed, it was at least a venial sin for us Catholics to go. Protestants or, as we used to call them, non-Catholics, had ministers.

Well, now that it has been at least grudgingly acknowledged that if Martin Luther hadn't bolted, he'd have a feast day in the Roman calendar, and now that we are (at least outside the Irish hierarchy) more charitably inclined toward our separated brethren, we shouldn't think this new usage of "ministry" sinister.

We should think it dumb.

Dumb because it upholds a vision of the church that is hallucinatory. This is not the fault of those who introduced the usage. Thomas F. O'Meara, in a fine

Finding Fault

book entitled *Theology of Ministry*, gives a rich and succinct definition of ministry. He calls it "the public activity of a baptized follower of Jesus Christ flowing from the Spirit's charism and an individual personality on behalf of a Christian community to witness to, serve, and realize, the kingdom of God."

But that is not, really, what the people who accept paychecks and prestige from ecclesial institutions mean when they talk about "ministry." And those are the people who talk about ministry most. What such people mean by ministry is, in fact, "that for which professional Christians are owed something."

The "something" is a sum of money, peer recognition, a "right," power within the community, a piece of the action, a title, an office, a means by which one person may assert authority and make that authority felt. Come to think of it, maybe we *should* consider that usage of "ministry" sinister. In any case, the activity it describes shouldn't be mislabeled. And these days it's often called Christian.

In fact, I don't think that "the public activity of a baptized follower of Jesus Christ" should look anything like what Church professionals call ministry. One of the truest ministers I've ever met is a wife and mother in South Bend, Ind. Underpaid for teaching local victims of the Reagan administration (unemployed or half-literate adults), frustrated by institutional indifference and mediocrity, and fiercely devoted to her students, she manages as well to adminis-

Michael O. Garvey

ter a household, care for her own and other's children and be present as Christ is present to an enormous variety of God's people.

Her "ministry" is done at the kitchen table, on the telephone and from the battered station wagon her family uses to get around. She hears confessions, gives counsel, encourages, criticizes, befriends, defends and denounces. People with and without formal religious vows, people broken by war and poverty, people harried by the confusion of marriage and childrearing, people with alcohol and drug problems and people with nothing in particular to do have been touched by her ministry.

Her ministry is most successful because she is pretty much unaware of it. So are those to whom she ministers. What her friends (not clients) honor in her is a valiant, mostly triumphant, and continued effort to see and love in other human beings what Christ sees and loves in them. A member of the young and laterally mobile urban professional class, she builds up the kingdom of God. She is a minister, but if you called her that, she'd throw you out of the kitchen, whether you had finished your beer or not. What she is is a Roman Catholic.

Adveniat Regnum Tuum

T HE OUTRAGES of the day are behind them; the post-dinner tootsie-roll overdose is behind them; the last shuddering spasm of sugar-induced hyperactivity is behind them; the tumult and shouting and the clangor of bath-time combat is behind them; they've finished watching some mind-eroding violence on the "A-Team" TV program. He has despaired of parenthood and is in full retreat before all that is wicked and seductive and implacable in contemporary culture.

As if to recoup losses, he reads to them from C.S. Lewis' subversively God-obsessed *Narnia Chronicles*, after which they stumble their collective and familial way through the Lord's Prayer. As he lingers, watching their consciousness evaporate beneath their childish fatigue, his kid-affected imagination trips over an artifact that had been gathering dust in some corner or another of his memory. A phrase in an ancient language from the prayer they have just recited together, his boys and he.

Adveniat regnum tuum.

As with other half-understood Latin words and phrases he'd picked up as an altar boy, it still glitters in his mind like some jewel. Long ago, it had struck him as a thick and shining tapestry of a phrase, redolent with incense and mystery; rich, obscure, challenging,

173

Michael O. Garvey

but trustworthy as the smell of toast in the morning. If you just plain *knew* that God was behind everything that is and might at any moment rise up starkly before you, the phrase felt particularly right, the kind of phrase for which a boy dazzled by the romance of infinity and imminence might be strongly tempted to throw away his life or run away from home or take some blood oath, maybe. A child could know things like that and become emboldened to generosity. If the certainty that God is at hand has never really left him, how has he, now entrusted with children of his own, become so craven and ungenerous?

Could a man restore the imagination and heart of his childhood? What had the word *"adveniat"* once meant? A fine name for a coal-black Pegasus with a mane like fire, he supposes, or for a dragon-prowed battle sloop shattering an onslaught of chrome-capped ocean waves into 10,000 diamonds apiece, or for a splendid, high-walled castle atop a mountain of glass in a land ruled by the most beautiful woman in the world. *Adveniat regnum tuum.* A phrase that had once made him want to do something very grand and dangerous. To hear it said or sung at Mass had made him feel as if he *were*, in fact, doing something grand and dangerous.

Of course, as he eventually learned, he was.

Years, sins and numerous distractions and betrayals later, as he tries to pray the same prayer, this time in English, with his own children at their bedtime, he wishes he could convey to them the sheer enormity of what they are doing. He strains after that ancient moment, or fusion of moments, in his own childhood when the promise of real adventure had seemed to glow beneath the repetition of liturgical formalities.

What are those words, he thinks, that you, as a child, have heard sung horribly off-key or muttered at auctioneer's velocity by such a sprawling variety of strangely garbed and occasionally just plain strange men? What were those priests and you and your family and friends and acquaintances and enemies all doing together as those words reverberated through the incense-beclouded and garishly designed interiors of old churches and through the resentments and fears of your heart and through the turbulence of your memory and through the futile preoccupations of your earliest imagination?

You were all addressing the very ground of your being. You were doing it timidly, of course, with all the reverent deference of a Latin subjunctive phrase. Latin in those days, though badly or barely understood, was not as dead and sterile a liturgical language as some folks seem now to suggest. He has always thought its usage a verbal way of taking off your shoes because you were on holy ground.

After all, to have the unmitigated audacity to say welcome to the author of the galaxies and of whatever it is that the galaxies themselves come from! To be sure, he does this because he has been taught that this is the proper thing to do. He is doing as he's been told by good people whom he loves, people who certainly

Michael O. Garvey

seem to believe in this God. But when he begins to think about the sort of being that God is alleged to be, such a welcome begins to seem comically superfluous. The ancient joke about the 2,000-pound gorilla: Where does the maker and master of all things seen and unseen sit? Anywhere he wants, obviously. He can explode suns and universes by stretching and yawning, eat whole histories sprinkled with epic poems for breakfast and daydream a world religion or two while he gardens his light-years. His kingdom will always go pretty much wherever he damn well wills it to go.

But his kingdom is not that crude. True, it approaches us all, even these prayed-out kids of his who have long since fallen asleep, by a kind of onslaught, and the incarnation is like some cosmic depth charge in the previously distracted tranquility of human history. This invading kingdom seems to depend upon the frailest of fifth columns, this weakly emotive and deeply personal impulse expressed by a subjunctive phrase. Thy kingdom come.

That intention is itself, he knows, part of the invasion, an instance of grace. But how softly it always seemed to come, stealing through man's soul like a rumor through a town, easy to miss.

He looks at sleeping children, wondering how he, or they, or anyone can really be rescued.

Because how can one honestly desire the coming of this kingdom, which is coming whether one likes it or not? In the window of a grungy storefront in a skid-

Finding Fault

row section of town, he has looked at a vulgar depiction of televangelical rapture. Miniature mushroom clouds, as if from tiny atomic bombs, rise above a crumbling urban landscape as most of a wretched and terrorized populace riots in the streets below. Above the radioactive fluff—born aloft on it in fact—looms a white-robed and emphatically Caucasian humanoid of indeterminable gender. It seems to be hurling lightning bolts, Zeuslike, with its left arm (whether these are causing the atomic explosions is unclear) while its right encircles the first arriving cluster from an upward spiraling stream of smiling and clearly saved, predominantly Caucasian men and women dressed in the fashions of North American suburbia after V-J Day and before the Inchon landing.

He remembers thinking that if this artist's distressingly popular vision were even close to accurate, then there is something colossally wrong with absolutely everything. Neither God nor his kingdom could possibly be like this. Could they?

Well, why couldn't they? Something upholds the vulgarly rendered hopes of this revolting artwork, and no matter how feeble the imagination of the artist, or how stultifying his expression, both have clearly been convulsed by real vision. "On earth, nations will stand helpless, not knowing which way to turn from the roar and surge of the sea."

In the story he has just finished reading to his boys, Aslan, the great lion and lord of Narnia, is reclaiming his own kingdom. A human child, Lucy, asks one of

Michael O. Garvey

Aslan's most loyal subjects whether this fierce lion might not be safe. The believer's reply, "Who said anything about safe? 'Course he isn't safe. But he's good."

It is Advent, the season of the coming of the Lord, and his desire is disorderly as his wits. He doesn't really want "good," but he does want "safe." He is, in fact, a citizen of a republic dedicated to safety. He has celebrated this citizenship tonight, tucking abed his treasured kids in a warm room in a snug house on a reasonably quiet street in a competently policed city in a comfortable nation corseted by relatively secure borders.

Above his house, threading their way through stars and probing with artificial vision the global horizons, his nation's cleverest satellites threaten instant and murderous retaliation for incoming Soviet missiles, in case some high-strung Russian sub commander finally flips out. A few blocks from his house, a squad car responsibly cruises the immaculately clean parking lot of an innocuously named and discreetly designed red brick building in which unbidden and incoming children may likewise be intercepted and destroyed. Night is creeping steadily across the wary northern hemisphere, and the clamorous and accusing poor keep their place, south of the equator. It is Advent, and all of this, along with a few billion interior and personal treacheries, his very Lord approaches, scornful of earth's cosmic burglar alarms and clumsily locked jail cells. An astonishing child who relentlessly penetrates

Finding Fault

the soul-devouring safety devices of a deranged and rapacious world. And of a coward's heart.

It is Advent, and his sleeping kids look so worthy of safety.

And so utterly vulnerable, too.

Like some barely noticed and inconveniently begotten Third World kid, born on the scruffy margins of world affairs, into some confused family living in some occupied and exploited town, to some uneducated and hastily married local girl who's used to being ostracized by the pious and leered at by a boorish foreign soldiery, God himself sneaks into his own conquered and enslaved world, a chump among chumps, loser among losers, a baby born to show us that we can never live until we have learned how to die.

God himself gooing, gawing, drooling, needing to suck teats and spit up and be wiped clean and bellow and be changed; sharing our animality and anguish, our crazy need to flout and fly from death; utterly vulnerable to and needing what's best and worst about us: our attentive company. Our capacity to choose—for no reason at all—to delight and delight in a newborn, any newborn at all, any gift at all, in fact. Does our ability to choose enchant him? Could he be as fascinated by danger and adventure as some Midwestern altar boy dazzled by the romance of a Latin phrase?

We seem to seduce our creator, who launches himself, for purest generosity, into a world of randomness and risk, among his wildest human creations, wild because human—intimidated by the arrogance of earth

Michael O. Garvey

and dung and death but perpetually inflamed with some of the divine ferocity and relentless love. Exhilarated by the hearty acquiescence of Mary, awed by the loyalty of Joseph, delighted by the exuberance of shepherds and the pilgrimage of Eastern kings, wary of Herod's assiduous agents in the countryside, surely God has blessed the disorder and frailty of this event, which shares with sin itself an atmosphere of recklessness. Here, trembling, we may glimpse how much like us he is and how much like him we are.

God *knows* how crazed and distracted and cowardly we are, the nervous father thinks as he listens to the breathing of his sleeping boys and longs for their safety. He knows because he's Emmanuel, God With Us—even more with us than we are with each other on this hair-trigger night—shivering beneath these murderous spacecraft and writhing hopelessly under the abortionist's blade, a victim of cluster bombs and leukemia, starvation and foolishness, torture and sensitivity sessions, ecclesial fatuity and human fright.

He knows our anxiety who has made himself, for love of us, unsafe from all assault. He knows our cowardice, whose own friends have fled when needed most. He knows our treason, whose imprisonment, torture and execution we allow and guarantee. It isn't surprising that he comes so stealthily, but that he comes exposed and helpless as these sleeping children can only be intended to break a man's heart. A person, a nation, a world have waited whole millennia for deliverance. Rescue us, Lord, they've prayed, from

180

Finding Fault

the necessity and meanness of our history and from the rapacity of this all-devouring earth and from the fatuity of our collective and individual self-righteousness and pride. And their prayer has been answered. Sort of.

We and our children are drowning, the father thinks, and God has thrown his own child into the waves with us. This is a complex reassurance.

A Season of Light

I F YOU haven't yet obtained your Advent wreath, you may be excused. Stop reading this immediately and go get or make one. You owe at least that much to your friends, your kids, your folks and yourself. You owe at least as much to anyone with whom you sit at table, even if you sit at table alone—which, in any case, we Christians all know is impossible: A person is never alone, only attentive or inattentive. A table set for one needs candles during Advent, too.

Catholicism, Christianity for that matter, is largely a matter of candles. At few times does that become as obvious as during this season, as children's eyes start marking the march of candlelight around the pinebough circle toward incarnation. Each week of Advent, the dinner table grows brighter with the additional candlelight, the light coming into the world.

There were eight children in the family that first taught me about Advent. Each Advent night before saying grace, we used to take turns lighting the wreath, one of us striking the match and igniting the wicks while another (after rebelliously muttering that it was really *her* turn to light the candles) would read from my mother's old St. Andrew's missal something like "O rising star, brightness of God's eternal light, sun of justice, do thou come and shed thy radiance upon us who languish in darkness and the shadow of death."

Finding Fault

There, surrounded by loved ones a few days before Christmas, a few minutes before a fine and noisy meal, eyes sparkling in the glow of a ring of candles and nostrils filled with the clean and implacable scent of evergreen, we would be reminded that we languished, really, in darkness and the shadow of death. Of course, like all good Catholic kids, we seldom paid attention to such readings, but every once in a while, a word or phrase would sink in and tease our imagination toward wonderment. A theology lesson might begin at bedtime, with some garbled question such as "Mom, what does 'the language of darkness' mean?"

But, however clumsily, the seed managed to get planted, and like all good Catholic kids, we grew up with deep suspicions about the world. The Latin and strange feast-keeping and black-clad effeminate men and ancient liturgies and, always the candles, reminding us that the world by itself was a dark and death-governed place. Advent, more than most seasons, was a time to remember that the world was a place that stood in desperate need of the light of the world.

Advent is a good time to remember that the Church is a counterculture, an underground, an outcast gypsy family. Our agenda calls for nothing less than God's repossession of the whole world, which is why, when we are at our very best, the world despises us. Advent is a good time to remember that our strategy is similarly uncomplicated: We carry throughout the universe the uncreated light that has been given to us at Christmas.

Michael O. Garvey

Perhaps we too often take for granted our desire for light. That desire is itself a gift, and we celebrate and give thanks for that gift during this season of desire. But we should be under no illusion about the world into which that light has come to rescue us. The world, if those who seem to control it provide a reliable index of affection, simply does not love light.

I'm not speaking metaphorically, either: The Air Force has tested the latest device to which it will confess—an antisatellite weapon—aboard an F-15 plane high above Edwards Air Force Base, firing a rocket "pointed," so a newspaper account says, "at the light emitted from a distant star." There have been three previous tests, during which the weapon has cruised distractedly around in space, one time assaulting a derelict satellite. But finally—and high time, too, when you think about it—the target is a star.

The absentminded permission we have given military technicians in pursuit of might will eventually kill us and our chidren. We'd rather it didn't, of course, but we are justifiably afraid that it will. After all, when you go about defending your freedom, containing belligerent Soviets, standing tall against Shi'ites, stimulating the economy, thwarting AIDS, creating jobs, upholding the sanctity of marriage, being realistic and all that, you are obliged to make unpleasant choices. If an annihilative technology is aimed at you, you need protection. It's an imperfect world, and you do the best you can.

But forget all that. A deeper purpose has begun to

Finding Fault

disclose itself. An unconscous logic may have determined the Pentagon's most recent target option. The idea is to bring down light itself. We must shoot down stars.

One crystal clear night not long before the Air Force had announced the first salvo in its war on starlight, I drove with friends a few miles out from South Bend, away from the glare of streetlights, to an open place with a generous view of unadulterated sky. One of my friends, an astronomer and meteorologist, had brought with him a powerful telescope through which we were able to see the moons of Jupiter and the rose deserts of Mars. He patiently traced the shape of Taurus until we could see it vaulting one horizon, and then showed us the complicated jewelry of the Pleiades, and then, across the sky from there, Sagittarius, showing how beyond that Archer, at a barely imaginable distance which it would take far longer than what we call human history to traverse, lay the heart of our galaxy.

It was dazzling. And as nearly always happens when people stare silently at stars for a very long time, someone mentioned that some of the stars we were looking at might not exist any longer, inviting us to think about how through the physical enormity of the universe, light races through space like a rumor, with a relentless and perhaps unchanging stride, but bringing only itself, only mystery. To think about light, especially starlight, is a message, a language, perhaps a hymn, but decidedly a gift. There on the surface of

185

Michael O. Garvey

that dark, wet field beneath an infinity of distant suns, it seemed such a privilege to be a man, to be a being worthy of beholding stars, to be a creature whose awe of failing starlight could give way to a craving for the source of all light, for the one who dwells in unapproachable light, for the one who is uncreated light.

It seemed that night that light was a sacred thing, the most immediate and arresting evidence that the universe was trying to tell us something—better, *was* telling us something that perhaps we were not yet worthy to hear. We had been told that Christ was our light; that we, the baptized, were the light of the world; that the word of the Lord was a light for our footsteps, that the Church, our society with Christ at its center, was a light for all the nations. How could we begin to understand what all these things meant without paying reverent attention to these splendid and implacable suns whose relentless shining perforated an infinity of nighttime?

No wonder the servants of that increasingly sophisticated technology through which death is most conspicuously worshiped in our time would intuit such a target. Almost as if in appeasement of the nihilistic God of their darkest imaginings, they now find themselves inattentively waging a futile war on light itself.

Advent is a good time to remember that they have been defeated already, and that uncreated light has arrived to destroy death and reclaim the world forever.

The Kindness of a Stranger

IT is Advent. His children now in bed, the man wonders.

What do you do when you're born in a fortress and you fear that the very ramparts that surround you and your family and your friends and your Church and yourself are themselves responsible for the ugliness of your predicament? What do you do when you begin to mistrust the motives and sanity of the priests and admen and experts and president and deal-makers and coattail riders who develop and recommend the intercontinental apocalypse repellants, the first-alert doctrinal screening systems and the state-of-the-art womb mines? Are these quite powerful people diabolically possessed? Are they any less obsessed by power and death than their foes are? Are you? Is there any room in this nest of preoccupations for a stranger, an uninvited guest, a baby—God?

He remembers a hike he once took through a desolate, nearly lunar Clare County landscape, how he'd clambered rock fence after rock fence of an apparently infinite matrix of flinty vacant lots, numbed by the sterility of the soil and the suggested ferocity and desperation of those generations of hard-scrabble farmers who had meticulously marked off tiny parcels of barren land to leave as worthless tokens, he supposed, to cherished children not so much unlike the two he's just prayed and read to sleep. It was a cheerless and alarming scene, which seemed to anticipate a time after the end of the world.

This is what a bomb-scraped Scarsdale or Glenview or Colorado Springs might be a thousand years in the wake of Armageddon, with no one to behold even its emptiness. And he remembers catching a glimpse of something bright and red as newly split blood deep in the interstices of those dead boulders and realizing with a shock, that he was looking at the earth's most durable and astonishing flowers at work—delicate, exquisite and implacable shoots that could lift half-acres in search of sunlight, flowers that could cleave whole rocks.

The Lord comes like those, too, he hopes. I have imagined, rather than been myself, letting my imagination and my fear and my appetite and ambition build up whole labyrinths of breastworks against the coming of this child, who may nevertheless break and break and break my heart until its stoniest resistance shatters and the blood of unadulterated life roars through my whole being in eucharistic torrents.

He picks up grotesque figurines from the toy-strewn floor—little boys' excuses for playing with dolls: a Nordic thug named He-Man, a double-headed bad guy named Two-Bad and a reptilian hybrid called Cobra-Cahn. Tossing the sinister dolls into their toy-box, he thinks about how any fear, a nation's fear of death, a couple's fear of children, even a child's fear of phantoms, can become a market, subtly consolidating

Finding Fault

the deathgrip on our hearts and imaginations by requiring our economic cooperation. (He has argued the point with his wife before: *Must* their kids play and even sleep with these god-damn Nazi santos? She, with preemptive and wifely wisdom, has agreed that their enthusiasm is unhealthy and has invited him to wean them from it. He, yielding in yet another battle, has capitulated to the Plastic Toy Pantheon.)

Good Lord, transform all things, he whispers, looking out the boys' bedroom window on an empty street. Transform my fear of you to dread and my dread to awe and my awe to longing, and let my longing become a sort of fifth column in preparation for your birth and assault. Let our family be a secret cell, and these babies agents; let our prayers be subversive; bless our fiercest sabotage of all that the world and its corporations, nations, armies, churches, endowments and boards of trustees hold dearest; smile on our betrayal of the republic of power, cowardice and necessity; endow us with that quiet and unique peace that splits rocks, breaks hearts and flattens empires, the peace of which you alone are guarantor. Come, Lord Jesus.

Watching his sleeping boys, he catches some of their fatigue. He has prayed a bit and grown tired even from that puny effort. He, too, will fall asleep this winter night in a warm house surrounded by the people he loves most, protected from everything he fears most by assured and regular wages and endless distractions and fitful sleep and brass locks and savvy statecraft and heavily patrolled borders and competent police forces and a well-equipped soldiery and well-deployed satellites and precision-tooled, nuclear-tipped missiles.

He and his children are safe from the onslaughts of hostile armies, safe from malevolent burglars, safe from the Third World cries of Lazarus, safe from all who are inconveniently and ill-begotten, safe from AIDS and rats and jailers and secret police and the Congregation for the Doctrine of the Faith and frivolous liturgies. Safe, in fact, from every imaginable distress except the child on whom he has called in prayer, who takes even a worried and insomniac father at his word. Who stalks a wounded and sinful heart with the relentlessness of a predator scenting blood. Who has come to inflict his peace on nations by doing battle with the very death nations have always needed to engender and uphold and worship. Who has come to reveal his Father's disconcerting nonchalance about, if not disdain for *realpolitik*, institutional order, personal convenience and mainstream opinion. His love is such that one wonders whether the mere world can bear it. No wonder one single spineless parent needs to beg his mercy.

But how beg mercy from a baby?

The story of his coming is deceptively familiar and so almost abstract. Remember, the father asks himself, when the abstract presence in your marriage shattered to become a baby, this little kid asleep in front of you? How you and your wife had known, of course, that

Finding Fault

she was pregnant and that this meant that a child, some child, "the baby," was approaching. How you'd both worried and wondered and been Lamazed and bewildered for month after month until that one chaotic and precarious night you had both feared might be your last together in this world. How a routine prenatal doctor's visit had given way to a frightening ambulance ride and an emergency surgery and a sprint down a labyrinth of fluorescent-lit corridors to an intensive care nursery, where you had finally held and—weeping with relief and terror and happiness and guilt and grief for the children who hadn't survived and those who had and those who had been murdered and betrayed and abandoned— beheld, not a baby, but this baby, not a child, but this heroically struggling three-and-a-half-pound boy, not somebody's child but your son, not expected but here.

The prison walls of your ego had been shattered in a split second by this unsolicited event over which you had absolutely no control. Death had closed in around your fledgling family and had been defeated, turned back and put to flight. Your wife would live, and the baby was no longer a baby, but this baby, this one, specific, particular, alarmingly premature, physically disadvantaged and distressingly emaciated little boy who had shown up too suddenly for anyone to invite him.

Something, a stranger, a person, *this* person, had crashed through all the small talk and apprehension and planning and tedium and dread. Now. You. Him.

Michael O. Garvey

Her. Us. Here. And so, like any sane man holding his baby in a universe that a birth had permanently and eternally altered, you were overwhelmed. As you held the baby as close as possible to the surgical mask they'd made you wear, a nurse dabbled the tears from your eyes with a cotton swab so that you could see your new son.

So, he supposes, must all hearts be convulsed and then broken if any of us is to behold the vulnerable Christ child, the true conqueror of the universe.

He kisses the boys while they sleep and looks again out the window where the darkness has deepened perceptibly. It is close to the winter solstice, and the sun had dropped about as far below the horizon as God allows it to, and soon, regardless of the world's predilections, it will begin to rise in its orbit, millisecond by millisecond gaining sovereignty over the darkness.

He has work to do. He must have candles ready near all the windows so that he can light them a few minutes before the children wake up, when he will lie to them, telling them they were lit all last night so that Jesus could find his way to their house. To get them, he will go downstairs to the kitchen, where his wife will be wrapping things in brightly colored paper, perhaps a few more of those plastic Nazi dolls the boys like so much, and they will arrange the presents around the tree and make ready a vast breakfast and begin with paper and tinfoil and plastic to transform the entire downstairs of the house into the gaudiest Disneyland the children have ever seen, and they

Finding Fault

might have a drink afterward and fall asleep with their arms around each other and then—many ages after the creation of the world when God in the beginning made the heavens and the earth, long after the flood, more than 4,000 years after Abraham's birth and 35 centuries after Moses led the children of Israel out of Egypt and about 3,000 years after David was anointed king and about 2,000 years after a baby came to rule the universe forever—their entire household being at peace, they will awaken, to welcome him, as if for the first time.

And this time, he vows, inhaling the strange and bracing aroma of fresh pine branches as he crosses the living room, this one time, not some time or next time, but *this* time, they will not neglect the surreptitious host of their party who has come as guest and giver to join them.

God in the Woods

WHILE trying to enter an abysmal housing project in the big city near here, an ambulance was recently pelted with stones and eggs. The paramedics fled and the child whose mother had called them died. The police were then summoned, arrived in force, and found the apartment after gingerly climbing five flights of unlighted stairs. The same sorts of people who throw stones at paramedics smash out lights in stairways and terrorize folks who try to use the elevators, which usually don't work anyway.

All of this will be dealt with in court. As will the case of a few bored adolescents, who, a few weeks earlier, had dropped a foot square slab of concrete from a highway overpass, shattering the windshield of a passing van and instantly decapitating a father of eight. According to reports, they were apprehended after bragging to other bored kids about how they'd offed somebody.

According to my niece, classmates in her high school have alleviated their boredom by taking and showing videotaped movies of other kids having oral sex with each other. On first hearing the story, I dismissed it as some adolescent exaggeration, designed to shock adults. But her parents, wonderful and by no means credulous people, believe it. So does a friend of mine, a devoted secondary school teacher who strug-

Finding Fault

gles to inspire hope among the most pathetic kids in our local public school system. "Civilization is ending," she says, without the slightest indication that she's kidding. The litany of the zeitgeist goes on and on, and one is tempted to believe that what is wrong with the universe is, well, us.

I think we're a lot of the problem, all right. A species that can produce tritium gas, Wheel of Fortune, the IUD and McDonald's hamburgers is a species you want to watch yourself around. But the disgusting social arrangements that can spawn such things are not rooted solely in our societies nor even in our souls. There's something every bit as wrong with the universe as there is with us.

The noise of December wind banging against our insulated house right now is also an admonition that this domestic coziness—the warm light of the kitchen, the mixed smells of baked bread, coffee and Advent wreath pine, the reassuring hum of the refrigerator and the confident, regular tick of the clock on the wall behind me as I write—that all of this is conditional stuff, and that the universe which surrounds it has a way of being brutal and unsparing. The snow which laces this wind is breathtaking to behold when the tawny light outside our backdoor window floods it. Last week, on the same night our community opened an efficient and hospitable shelter, an area froze to death in precisely this beautiful snow. When your wife and children are nestled all snug in their beds, and you're alone with your thoughts in the kitchen and you hear that relentless wailing, you know how much of creation theology is bull. We are, in fact, strangers here, and our place in this continuum of material and mortality is provisional.

Perhaps this is only a dark mood brought about by a recent reading of one of the haunting stories in our region: Only some three hundred years ago, in just this sort of weather and not very far from here, the French explorer La Salle returned to a fort he'd established in the Illinois country the previous year and with unwitting irony named Broken Heart, to discover that his men had mutinied and vanished into the wilderness. Amidst the rubble of that abandoned camp at Creve Coeur, La Salle found no trace of them other than a charred piece of board on which someone had scrawled, " Nous sommes tous sauvages." ("We are all savages.")

About three hundred years later, in a high-tech, antiseptic, fluorescent-lit hospital which has since built on that site, I watched in helpless anguish as well-trained doctors and nurses rushed to save the lives of my wife and prematurely born son. Had nature been allowed to take its course, the Midwestern soil would have claimed what I love for fertilizer. All mankind is grass indeed, and they last no longer than a flower of the field.

Yesterday, I went for a walk with the same son to explore a tract of Indiana woodland. It is a fairly small, youngish forest which was once wilderness, then farmland, and is now broken, but emerging wil-

Finding Fault

derness once again. About a hundred feet off the path, we noticed the wreck of a schoolbus, a relic of the mid-1950s, incongruous among a thick stand of poplars and covered with obscene graffiti spraypainted in garish red. It must have been left there before the trees grew up around it. "Let's have a look," I suggested. He said he didn't really feel like it.

His voice had registered on an octave unnaturally low for him, and his nonchalance seemed pronounced. I think we both sensed his real dread of approaching this weird thing we'd found deep in the woods. There was boy-fright in his tone, as if his imagination had gone a little jittery on him. Anyone who has been a child knows what was going on: There might be a body in there. Or a woods monster. Fugitive and murderous river pirates with hatchets. A crazy, cackling old man with long white hair, red beady eyes and pointed teeth. Might be some thing you dimly remembered from a nightmare. Or savages.

I had to have a look at that bus. To do otherwise— to pretend that I didn't really feel like it either—would have been a conspicuous condescension, precisely the sort of thing that stings a kid like him. How about if he waited on the path? I asked. I'd be right back. "Cool," he said gruffly. "Besides, you'll be able to see my red snowsuit if you need to find me." I left him on the path, began threading my way through the snowdrifts and brush, and heard him call a last time. "Hey Dad. I'll be *right* here." Cool, I said.

Without a gloriously imaginative eight-year-old

boy there to interpret it, the schoolbus really wasn't much. Cursorily, I stuck my head into the frame of one of its shattered windows. More graffiti inside, much broken glass, no seats, ancient acorns and dead leaves. Someone, it seemed, had once attempted to set the thing afire. Turning, I began to retrace my steps to the footpath.

For what must have been about twenty seconds, I couldn't see my son. And for what seemed far longer than twenty seconds, my mind and heart and gut filled with a psychogenic torrent carrying every inarticulable fear a parent ever had for a child. He'd been swallowed by the woods and snow. Kidnappers. Wild dogs. Crashing timber. Savages. Now trying to keep my own voice natural, I called out into the seamless paisley of forest. "Hey, wave or something, so I can see you." Nothing. I called his name sharply and heard the peculiar expression of my own fright. "Hey, I'm right here, Dad!" The paisley opened enough to reveal, only a few feet in front of me, a startled and splendid eight-year-old towhead in a red snowsuit. But he'd heard the fear in my voice, too. We stayed close together and walked home quietly.

For a few moments, my son and I had a glimpse of the thing in the Midwestern forest which might have devoured the French mutineers at Creve Coeur, the thing which had inspired a deranged explorer to scrawl We Are All Savages as a sort of surrender to the surrounding wilds. The thing whose claim on his mother and himself had been broken eight years ago in a

Finding Fault

Peoria hospital by the genius of technology and the mystery of grace.

In a poem entitled "To Elsie," William Carlos Williams wrote about that thing, seen in the despair of a New Jersey cleaning woman, "as if the earth under our feet/ were/ an excrement of some sky/ and we degraded prisoners/ destined/ to hunger until we eat filth/ while the imagination strains/ after deer/ going by fields of goldenrod in/ the stifling heat of September/somehow/ it seems to kill us."

Oh sure, what God has created, God loves, and God's love makes sacred what God loves. But so much more than that needs to be said and pondered and beheld and suffered. The earthquake in already bleeding Armenia didn't take place because of any systemic injustice. Nor did the hurricane which flattened the already hopeless villages of Nicaragua. Nor did the floods in Bangladesh. When Mount St. Helens burst like a boil on the earth's skin, the gas suffocated a family or two. I remember a dead little boy in the back of his parents' pickup truck. The photographs of his corpse showed the eyes wide open and the mouth agape. A tiny and bewildered face stared into an empty sky, the place children always look for God.

Recently, when a green hickory branch broke and fell in the Illinois country, shattering the skull and mind and family and friends of a four-year-old boy below, the problem was not human hardness of heart. When leukemia was diagnosed in a six-year-old girl, her parents learned something no liberation theo-

Michael O. Garvey

logian has yet expressed about the nature of evil. None of these things is our fault.

There are those who have gazed unflinchingly at these things and said they are the will of God. Some unfathomable thing goes on, they seem to say, which makes sense out of our orphans, puts all our shattered children and demented and despairing parents into some context. It has to do with Jesus on the cross or multinational corporations or Our Lady of Fatima. Their assertions are duplicitous or insane.

No, a universe in which such things can happen is simply intolerable. And we have to tolerate it. The attempt to explain away such things is contemptible. And we can't help but try. The Faith makes no such attempt, but does enigmatically insist that God Himself has entered and overcome the horrors of this plainly blighted project. That He suffers with and in our flesh. That is no exhaustive reassurance, to be sure. In fact, it is a suggestion that the Father Jesus reveals in the parable of the Prodigal Son is an even stranger figure than the relentlessly generous old guy in the story. It is an awesome thing to hear Christian theologians use the word "incarnation" as if they knew what they were talking about. It's a word that strains after a crucial and elusive astonishment, a thing so profound that one can only yearn for it, much as a panic-stricken man might yearn to see a flash of familiar red nylon fabric in the woods.